Practical Pre-School

Help your child to learn

Contents

Personal, Social and Emotional Development

Making friends	6
Taking turns and sharing	7
Thinking of others	8
Finding out about feelings	9
Saying sorry with a hug	10
When someone dies	11
Learning social skills	12
Saying please and thank-you	13
Learning about rules	14
Learning right from wrong	15
Washing hands	16
Mealtime manners	17
Getting dressed	18
Everyone's a winner!	19
Talking in a group	20
Likes and dislikes	21
Sons and daughters	22

Communication, Language and Literacy

Making time to read together	24
Understanding stories	26
Jack and the Beanstalk	27
Incy Wincy Spider	28
Telling tales	29
Using your local library	30
Making books together	31
Finding out about phonics	32
Name games	33
Learning to listen	34
Rhyming pairs	35
What's in a name?	36
Words and pictures	37
Time for talk	38
First stages of writing	39
'I can write like mummy'	40
Making a scrap book	41
Help your child to think	42

Mathematical Development

What we mean by number	44
Counting at home	45
Make your own number frieze	46
Rhymes and stories	47
Play your cards right	48
Trucks and trains	49
Letterbox game	50
A mathematical treasure hunt	51
What is sorting?	52
Sort the socks	53
Going on a bear trail	54
You've grown!	55
Making maths fun	56
Washing day maths	57
Maths in the kitchen	58
It's time to tidy up!	59
The language of time	60
Exploring space and movement	61
Sam the very silly snake	62
Learning about shape	63
Patterns with shapes	64
Make a shape mobile	65
Makea pyramid	66

Knowledge and Understanding of the World

Stop, look, listen!	68
The Green Cross Code	69
Feely games	70
What do we mean by science?	71
What melts?	72
The world around us: forces	73
Finding out about materials	74
Finding out about reflections	75
The magic of magnets	76
Messing about with water	77
Floating and sinking	78
Making things from junk	79
Taking the lid off things	80
Learning to solve problems	81

Contents

Knowledge and Understanding of the World

Playing and learning	82
Learning about colour	83
Colour your conversation	84
The great outdoors	85
Getting back to nature	86
How does your garden grow?	87
Get into gardening	88
Finding out about plants and animals	89
All creatures great and small	90
Make a bird feeder	91
Marking time	92
When I was young	93

Physical Development

Learning what bodies can do	95
Going on a bear hunt	96
Learning words for actions	97
Learning to balance	98
Goldilocks and the three bears	99
Party game	100
Make a simple parachute	101
Hoop fun	102
Ball games	103
Playing catch	104
Happy hands	105
Simon says	106
Using hands and fingers	107
Cleversticks	108
Recipe for playdough	109
Feeling good and keeping healthy	110
Learning how our bodies work	111
Getting the best from ride-on toys	112
Scissor happy	113

Creative Development

From scribble to drawings	115
Drawing what you see	116
Brush strokes	117
Printing with paints	118
Using wax crayons	119
Make a collage	120
Fun with glitter and glue	121
Puppets for fun	122
The wonders of wood	123
Sowing the seeds of creativity	124
Making a sea-shell plaque	125
Sweet dreams	126
Buttons to bake	127
Making music	128
Make your own drum	130
One, two, three, four, five	131

Starting school

How to help your child	133
Preparing for playtime	134
A guide to baseline assessment	135

While we have made every effort to contact people whose articles are featured in this book, we apologise if any authors have not been notified.

Published by Step Forward Publishing Limited
25 Cross Street, Leamington Spa CV32 4PX
Tel: 01926 420046

www.practicalpreschool.com

© Step Forward Publishing Limited 2005
Illustrations by Cathy Hughes

All rights reserved. No part of this publication may be reproduced, stored in a retrieval system, or transmitted by any means, electronic, mechanical, photocopied or otherwise, without the prior permission of the publisher.

ISBN-10: 1-902438-83-3   ISBN-13: 978-1-902438-83-2

All material has been published previously in *Practical Pre-School,* a monthly magazine for early years education professionals. With thanks to the following writers:

Mary Adossides, Ruth Andrews, Cath Arnold, Marie Ashford, Keeva Austin, David Bartlett, Ros Bayley, Lisa Bessinger, Chrys Blanchard, Carol Boylin, Steve Brookes, Lesley Button, Emily Cannon, Lynne Cashmore, Rona Catterall, Ann Clay, Elizabeth Coller, Naomi Compton, Joan Craven, Carole Creary, Ursula Daniels, Shirley Davison, Debbie Denham, Rubina Din, Collette Drifte, Margaret Edgington, David Elcome, Judith Elkin, Jean Evans, Sue Fisher, Lorraine Frankish, Barbara Garrad, Janet Gilbert, Jo Graham, Alison Grant, Judith Harries, Karen Hartley, Sue Hedley, Linda Henderson, Gill Hickman, Vicky Hislop, Penny Holland, Anne Hunter, Karen and Matthew Jarvis, Rose Johnson, Caroline Jones, Cameron Kathini, Chris Macro, Caroline McAdam, Maureen Mercer, Jane Moran, Julie Mountain, Sue Pearce, Sue Peasgood, Joan Santer, Nanette Smith, Rachel Sparks Linfield, Judith Stevens, Sara Stocks, Rebecca Taylor, Pam Taylor, Helen Tovey, Belle Wallace, Hilary White, Rhona Whiteford, Gay Wilson, Kate Wright.

Introductions to chapters:
Beth Casey and Caroline Jones

Introduction

Helping your child

You are your child's first and most important teacher. All the time you spend with them – reading, playing or just talking – they are learning. Everyday activities which to you seem ordinary can to your child be a wonderful experience and an opportunity to explore and discover. Learning needn't be – and shouldn't be – a chore. It should be something you can share and enjoy together. The activities in this book may seem like games but they also have clear educational objectives – so have fun and learn at the same time!

Early learning

Whether your child goes to a pre-school, nursery or daycare setting or is in a Reception class in a primary school, if they are aged between three and five then the activities they do will have been specially planned to help them achieve particular goals or outcomes.

In England, the Early Learning Goals set out what most children should have achieved by the end of the Foundation Stage. The Foundation Stage runs from when a child is three to the end of their first year of compulsory schooling (Reception class). Don't expect your child to be achieving these goals when they are still in pre-school, aged three or four, as they will still be working towards them.

All children develop at different rates and the children in your child's group or class will probably be working at different levels. Their teacher will be observing and assessing them all the time, helping them to progress. They will plan and provide suitable activities and experiences to support the learning needs of your child.

The power of play

Some of these activities will be play-based but that doesn't make them any less valuable. Some of the best learning takes place when children have the freedom to explore, discover – and have fun – without an adult telling them what to do or think. Because playing is fun it is easy to forget its educational value, but play can be a powerful tool for learning.

How children learn

The Early Learning Goals cover six areas. These are:

- Personal, Social and Emotional Development
- Communication, Language and Literacy
- Mathematical Development
- Knowledge and Understanding of the World
- Physical Development
- Creative Development

This does not mean that children learn in separate areas. Your child may be playing with their toy cars and garage: they will be talking, handling the cars, and maybe sorting the cars and lorries and pretending to fill them up with petrol. Your child will be developing socially by sharing, talking and interacting; and being creative by imagining they are playing in a real garage. At the same time they could be developing mathematical skills by lining up the cars and counting them.

You may notice that your child is developing more quickly in one area than another. Three-year-old Joshua, for example, is a confident speaker but needs more support in his social development as he finds it hard to share. Grace, who is four, concentrates for long periods and enjoys books. Her language is well developed, but she lacks confidence in physical activities and needs encouragement to use climbing equipment.

The activities in this book have been grouped into chapters which correspond to the six areas of learning. At the beginning of each chapter we give a few examples of what you might expect to see your child doing at various stages of development but every child develops at a different rate. Remember that developmental milestones are a useful guide but childhood is a journey, not a race.

Across the UK

There are different Government guidelines for education in Wales, Scotland and Northern Ireland but they have many similarities. They may use different words or the same words in a different order but the expectations are basically the same.

Personal, Social and Emotional Development

This is about children's attitudes to learning, how they see themselves, how they relate to people – other children and adults - and their behaviour. It also covers how they care for themselves and their sense of community.

- By the end of the Reception class year a child should be motivated and interested to learn but still want to find out more. A three-year-old will show they are curious by constantly asking questions or repeatedly asking 'Why?' They may touch and interfere with things in shops. An older child will want to explore, experiment and talk about what they've seen or done.

- A young child might be at the stage of snatching toys or squabbling but will gradually learn to share, for example, by offering another child a pretend cup of tea when they're playing.

- A young child may still need help washing their hands, going to the toilet or putting on their coat, but as their self-care skills develop they will be able to dress and undress independently and manage their own personal hygiene.

Help your child to learn

Relationships are about communication, about children feeling they belong and recognising their lives are connected with other people. A child who is able to form effective relationships will grow up to be a secure, sensitive and caring adult

Making friends

- Children can learn to recognise and relate to familiar adults and other children from an early age. Try to encourage this by joining a local parent and toddler group or going to organised activities such as swimming.

- Encourage other children and adults to visit your home from time to time and accept invitations to go to other people's houses.

- Look after someone else's child for a short period to encourage them to play together.

- Go on outings to the park or for a walk with a friend.

- Point out the adults working in shops and talk about them to your child. Encourage your child to make eye contact with these adults, for example, handing over the money to pay for the goods - and at the same time having the confidence to say 'hello'. This is also a good time to remind them that it is good manners to say 'please' and 'thank-you'.

- Encourage familiar adults and older children to share books on a one-to-one basis with your child.

- Use photographs to talk about people in your child's life. Make a book called 'My Friends' or 'My Family' to help them understand the idea of belonging to a group.

- Play games with your child and become involved in their imaginative play.

- Let your child help with chores around the house.

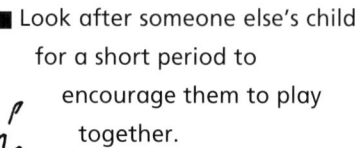

Taking turns doesn't come naturally to young children - it is something they learn. You can help your child by playing turn taking games at home. Here are some ideas

Taking turns and sharing

Even small babies take turns in communicating with their parents. If you talk to your baby you'll soon realise that they respond in some way each time you speak to them. Games such as 'peek a boo' which they copy will encourage the idea that someone else does something 'And then it's my turn!'

Toys to swap
Children can be possessive of their toys. Try to encourage children to play with one of each other's toys at the same time, returning them after a set time.

Lead by example
Join in with your child's role play and take it in turns to be the cook or do the washing up. Point out when adults are taking turns - 'It's Daddy's turn to do the cooking/washing up today'.

Go to a local parent and toddler group. Don't give up going because your child is always in the middle of a fight over a toy! He's learning to take turns.

Helping at home
At meal times, encourage children to pass plates around to other family members. Let them help with setting the table - one child can put out the cutlery, another the plates or the tomato ketchup. (If you have one child, you or another adult will have to take turns with them.)

Point out the turn taking as you post letters in the post-box, feed the rabbit or water the plants.

Songs and rhymes
Sing nursery songs and rhymes involving two people taking turns, for example 'Two little dickey birds' or 'Jack and Jill'.

Share the shopping
Shopping with young children can be made more enjoyable if they have a job to do. Perhaps they can put the tins in the trolley while you put in the packets.

Using the right words
Try to use words which help children understand the idea of turn taking:
'It's not your turn yet, but it will be in a minute'.
'Whose turn is it to lay the table today? Yes, it's your turn, Simon. Jennie had a turn yesterday.'
'One at a time!'
'Take it in turns - Katie first, then William.'
'Don't worry, you'll all have a turn!'
When children are playing and you hear them saying to each other 'No, it's his turn now', then you know they've got the idea. But, remember, even teenagers still argue about whose turn it is to sit in the front of the car!

Perhaps the greatest way of encouraging and teaching your child to develop caring and sharing attitudes is by example. It is a case of 'Do as I do' as well as 'Do as I say'

Thinking of others

Caring and sharing
If you are going to phone or write to a grandparent or elderly relative, involve your child. Give a simple explanation - Grandma is all by herself, shall we send her a card/letter?

If you decide to visit a new neighbour, again a simple explanation involves your child and sows the seeds of thoughtfulness - 'The new family don't have any friends here. Shall we go and say hello?'.

Sharing thoughts is important on a personal level, too. If a child is unwell, you care for them. If you feel unwell, tell your child - 'I have a headache, will you look after me today by playing quietly or tidying up?'. Far better to encourage care than to snap or become irritable when the child does not understand why.

Give praise
It is important to build a child's self-esteem, so if your child does something which is caring or helpful then praise them.

If a child is not so good at sharing or taking turns, maybe with a younger member of the family, then try the 'I understand' approach. 'I understand that you want . . . but if you wait until . . . has finished then you may have your turn'. This applies to sharing toys, demanding attention and interrupting conversations. Reinforce this response by giving attention/the toy at the appropriate time.

Christmas time
As Christmas draws near, children become excited at the thought of presents. If your child wants to write a letter to Father Christmas of the 'I would like' variety, you could spend time together writing a second list - what would other people really like? Not material gifts but something more thought provoking, such as 'Aunty would like someone to visit ...', 'The lady next door would like us to be quieter ...'

Clear away unwanted toys to make room for new. Why not sort out items in a reasonable condition - toys, outgrown clothes - and let your child go with you to the local charity shop or Christmas appeal? Explain how either the gifts or funds are used to help less fortunate people.

Involve your child in your Christmas preparations. Could they choose which card to send to Grandpa or spend time drawing a special picture to enclose? Could they help prepare the mince pies and take them with you to an elderly neighbour?

Suggest positive ways of showing how we care. Hugs and cuddles may have high priority, but putting away toys, sharing and getting ready for bed without a fuss all show consideration, too. If a child develops a sense of responsibility and understanding within the family then this is continued in the outside world.

Try a bedtime 'What did I do that was kind today' conversation. Talk about what you could do tomorrow.

What I did to help today
Colour the face

☺ I posted a letter for the neighbour

☺ I was quiet when my brother was asleep

☺ I took granny a picture

Name ....

There is no magic recipe to help your child be happy but parents who talk to their child and tune into their feelings provide the kind of 'emotional coaching' which is invaluable

Finding out about feelings

Before children can learn to control their feelings they need to know how to name and recognise them.

Sharing a family album or magazine pictures and talking about the faces and expressions can be a valuable experience. Children are fascinated by pictures and photographs of people and will spend a long time looking at them.

Cut out pictures from magazines together and talk about how the person in the picture is feeling and why that might be.

Remember, you know your child best. You can read their facial expressions and body language. Often you know how your child is feeling even when they can't find the words to tell you.

Telling them what you notice can be helpful. 'I noticed you frowning - are you feeling worried?' (rather than 'You're frowning - you must be worried') 'I heard you stamping upstairs - is there anything wrong?' (rather than 'Why are you so mad?').

Children have the right to express both positive and negative emotions. It can improve their confidence in themselves and in the relationships they form throughout life.

Children who are supported by people who love them are better at handling their own emotions, better at soothing themselves when they're upset and get upset less often. Their stress levels are low, they are in better physical health, have fewer behaviour problems and are more popular with their peers.

Family arguments can make everyone at home miserable, especially if children don't know how to say sorry for their own behaviour. Here's how to help ease the tension

Saying sorry with a hug

When there has been an argument at home between brothers and sisters or parent and child, for whatever reason, everyone ends up feeling bad and saying sorry is a good way to start resolving a situation. If that can be done with a hug or cuddle most children will feel the reassurance they need that they are forgiven.

Try not to go to sleep with unresolved anger or guilt. Sharing a quiet moment together before bed is a good time to talk about things that have happened during the day. You may need to help your child imagine how it would feel to be the person they have hurt. It is important to help children to say sorry to each other and to be prepared to apologise to them when you do things wrong.

Share this rhyme with your child. Can you think of any more misdemeanours to make up a new verse together!

Useful story books

Picture books are really useful for encouraging children to talk about their feelings and how to cope with them.

■ *I'm Sorry* by Sam McBratney (Collins)

By the author of *Guess How Much I Love You*, this picture book sensitively tells the story of a friendship between two young children who play together happily until one day they have an argument.

■ *Sorry, Miss!* by Jo Furtado and Frederic Joos (Andersen Press)

This funny tale tells of how a book takes a whole year to make its way back to the library, with the excuses growing more inventive and hilarious by the month.

■ *Lucy's Quarrel* by Jennifer Northway (Scholastic)

A realistic story about two friends who quarrel and refuse to make up. An everyday situation which many children will recognise and sympathise with - and there is a happy ending!

Sorry Mum, sorry Dad,
I didn't mean to be so bad.
I didn't mean to kick the cat.
I didn't mean to lose my hat.

Sorry Mum, sorry Dad,
I didn't mean to make you mad.
I didn't mean to drop my plate.
I didn't mean to make you late.

Sorry Mum, sorry Dad,
I didn't mean to make you sad.
Tomorrow I'll be really good,
Just like you always said
I should!

At some stage you may need to help your young child cope with losing a relative, friend or pet. Story books can be a helpful prop when helping children recover from the loss of someone close

When someone dies

Pets
It's important to be honest with children about the life-span of pets, especially hamsters and gerbils, as they often only live for two or three years. Losing a pet is often a child's first experience of death but it can be intense. They need lots of opportunities to talk about how they feel and share memories. It may help to have a simple service to say goodbye. Don't dismiss your child's grief. Help them to express it.

Some children can seem quite callous about the death of a pet and after a very short time are asking for a new kitten. Again, this is normal and should not be condemned.

■ Read *Frog and the Birdsong* with your child. This story is a matter-of-fact introduction to the death of a bird. The animals who have enjoyed the blackbird's singing choose to bury the bird and they feel sad. Then life returns to normal and they begin to play and have fun again.

Relatives
When a grandparent or close relative dies, young children are often confused and bewildered by their own feelings and the grief of those around them. They might ask repeated questions and need lots of reassurance. It is important to be as honest as you can when answering them. Many young children confuse death with sleep and you need to help them realise that there is a difference even if it is painful. It often helps children to be involved in some way in saying goodbye at a funeral service or other ritual. You may choose to compile a special book of photos and memories for your child to keep.

■ *Come Back, Grandma* is a sensitive story about a young girl who really misses her grandma. It talks honestly about the different answers you might give to a small child about what happens after death.

Books to read
Frog and the Birdsong
by Max Velthuijs
Red Fox
ISBN 0 0998 1780 2

Come Back, Grandma
by Sue Limb
Red Fox
ISBN 0 0992 1951 4

Badger's Parting Gifts
by Susan Varley
Collins
ISBN 0 0066 4317 5

Will my Rabbit go to Heaven?
by Jeremie Hughes
Lion
ISBN 0 7459 1221 4

When the World was New
by Alicia Garcia de Lynam
Lion
ISBN 0 7459 4271 7

Non-fiction
When People Die
by Sarah Levete
Watts
ISBN 0 7496 2817 0

What do we Think about Death?
by Karen Bryant-Mole
Wayland
ISBN 0 7502 2208 5

Friends
Children occasionally have to face the death of a friend or sibling. Again, it is important to give children the chance to talk about their memories, draw pictures, and be involved in saying goodbye.

■ In the picture book, *Badger's Parting Gifts*, Badger's friends think they will be sad forever. But gradually they are helped to remember him with joy and to treasure the gifts he left behind for each of his special friends.

This finger rhyme helps teach about good manners but also develops language skills

Learning social skills

Two fat gentlemen
Met in a lane

Bowed most politely
And bowed once again

And said 'How do you do?'

And 'How do you do?'

And 'How do you do?' again.

Repeat, replacing 'Two fat gentlemen' with:

Two thin ladies	*This time bend the forefinger*
Two tall policemen	*This time bend the middle finger*
Two small schoolboys	*This time bend the third finger*
Two little babies	*This time bend the little finger*

How this activity can help your child

- Children socialise with others as they do finger play.

- Rhyming and repetition is important for helping children learn to read.

- Following the sequence of events - working from thumb through to little finger - uses short-term working memory, another vital skill for reading. (When you read a sentence you need to be able to remember the words at the start by the time you get to the end in order to understand the meaning.) Building up patterns of rhymes helps children retain the information that has gone before.

- The rhyme is about saying hello politely. Children need to learn social skills and understand that we all behave according to a socially acceptable code of behaviour.

- The finger movements encourage dexterity and fine motor skills.

Learning to say please and thank you can be confusing for a child. Here are some ideas on how to encourage good manners

Saying please and thank you

To encourage good manners you should start by setting a good example, but even then children can be confused by what some of the 'magic' words mean. They sometimes find it difficult to reply to the question, 'What do you say?'. We've all seen a child desperately trying to remember which special word or phrase is required ('sorry', 'please', 'thank you', and so on) and almost inevitably say the wrong one. It needs to become second nature and only lots of practice will help.

Try learning this fun rhyme with your child to remind them to say please. You can sing it to the tune of 'Old Macdonald' (first four lines):

Feeling thirsty, need a drink?
Don't forget to say please.
Want some more, stop to think,
Don't forget to say please.

Feeling hungry, need some food?
Don't forget to say please.
Want some more, don't be rude,
Don't forget to say please.

Thank-you letters
It's good to get into the habit of saying thank you and it can be done in lots of imaginative ways. When your child goes to a friend's house to play or for a birthday party, remind them to be polite and say thank you. Older children may like to write a simple thank-you note or draw a picture.

Sometimes we give people cards or gifts to say thank you and home-made ones are often the best. Help your child to think of someone they would like to thank today and make a special card or some home-made sweets!

Useful story books

I Want My Dinner by Tony Ross (Collins): The little princess tries to learn some manners but once she's mastered 'please' and 'thank you', she finds others are not so polite.

Max and the Magic Word by Colin and Jacqui Hawkins (Puffin): Max's friends have to teach him polite behaviour.

The Bad-Tempered Ladybird by Eric Carle (Puffin): the bad-tempered ladybird is very rude and always trying to start a fight. Eventually, he learns it is better to be polite.

The Elephant and the Bad Baby by Elfrida Vipont (Puffin): a lovely rhythmic story about a bad baby who never says 'please'.

'Excuse Me' - Learning about Politeness by Brian Moses (Wayland): full of everyday situations, a child is helped to answer the question - how polite are you?

Thank-you sweets - Mint crunch bites
300g soft margarine
150g dark chocolate
2 tablespoons of water
100g crushed digestive biscuits
1/4 teaspoon of peppermint essence

Melt together the margarine, chocolate and water. Add the biscuits and flavour. Leave to cool. Roll into a sausage shape and wrap in clingfilm. Leave in the fridge overnight. Cut into discs and half-dip into melted chocolate. Put in sweet cases and say thank you with a smile.

Rules help children to understand about right and wrong but they must be based on good reasons. Children need the chance to talk about these reasons so that they come to understand why decisions have been made

Learning about rules

Children are encouraged to understand the difference between right and wrong at nursery and school and rules focus on the right behaviour wherever possible. Some of the things your child may have learned are shown in the boxes.

You might find it helpful to do this for home. Can you both draw pictures about the right and wrong things to do at home? Perhaps think of one example for each room in the house. Help your child by writing what each picture is showing and remember always to explain the reasoning behind what is right and what is wrong. For example:

In the kitchen
We do not touch the oven because . . .

In the bathroom
We should wash our hands after using the toilet because . . .

At the sand tray we don't throw sand or knock down someone else's sandcastle.

Outside we learn to wait our turn for the bikes and not argue about who goes on them first.

In the home corner we share the plates and cutlery, making sure everyone is able to join in.

You help your child to learn right from wrong by providing a home environment that encourages sound moral values. Here are some situations when you can encourage your child to think about the right way to behave

Learning right from wrong

Give your child the chance to make choices and decisions about daily events, such as:

Play time
Our friends are coming round to play. What are we going to do? We are going to share our toys and games and be kind to each other

- Give children the chance to solve problems for themselves. If discipline is too strict, children will not know how to act on their own.

- Help your child understand the consequences of their actions by talking about the outcome and suggesting ways in which it could be better.

Bed time
It's bed time - so what do we do now? We tidy away our toys so that we know where they are. We have a wash, clean our teeth and put on our pyjamas.

Getting ready to go out
What is the weather like? What do we need to put on? Do you need a coat? Wellies? A hat and gloves?

Play the 'If' game
If we go to our friend's house ... what do we do and think?
How do we behave? How do we treat others around us?

If we go shopping ... what do we do and think? How do we behave? How do we treat others around us?

If we go to the library ... what do we do and think?
How do we behave?
How do we treat others around us?

- Use different scenarios and situations. Encourage your child to think about the best way to react in each different situation.

- Recognise when your child has shown positive social attitudes. If they have shared their toys, played fairly or helped a friend give them lots of praise and reward.

Handwashing is one of those chores that young children find hard to understand. As they can't see germs they can't understand why it is so important. Here are some simple steps to teach your child how to wash their hands properly

Washing hands

Hands are one of the main ways of passing bacteria to food. This can cause food poisoning. Hands are also responsible for spreading viruses.

Many infections are passed to children from animals, especially pets. Dogs and cats can carry salmonella in their gut and because of the way they clean themselves these bacteria are also in their mouths. So try to make sure your child doesn't let animals lick them and get them to wash their hands after stroking or handling pets.

Here are some ways to help your child learn to wash their hands properly:

■ Make taps easy to turn on and off.

■ Make sure the soap bar is not too large for small hands to hold and that it is not cracked or dirty.

■ Make sure your child can reach the basin - provide a step if needed.

■ Protect them from burns - make sure the hot water is not too hot.

A few fun activities might encourage your child to wash their hands more often:

■ Make a poster together about washing hands and hang it in the bathroom as a reminder.

■ Buy some special bars of soap - animals or fruit shapes for example or soap with a small present in the centre which can only be reached after using up the soap.

■ Make a star chart and give stars when handwashing is remembered or done properly, with a small present after five stars.

Coming together to share a meal is not only about eating but about making time to sit down and talk as a family group. But mealtimes can be fraught and stressful if young children don't know what is expected of them or how to behave

Mealtime manners

Every family has its own way of doing this but you might find the following guidelines helpful. They are similar to the ones used by many nurseries and schools and so the ideas should not be new to your child.

- Decide what your rules are and try to stick to them!

- Wash hands before eating.

- Have as many meals sitting up to a table with your child as possible and encourage them to follow the family's manners.

- Praise your child's successes, for example when they manage a set of cutlery well.

- Try to play down the accidents and mistakes. Spilling things is perfectly normal for this age group. (Plastic table coverings make it easier to clear up.)

- Include your child when you have visitors, especially at lunch time visits as this is a great learning experience.

- Avoid giving your child snacks for at least an hour before meals.

- Don't have meals when your child is too tired.

- Encourage your child to be as independent as possible, feeding them may well be quicker but it will set them back in the long run.

Practise these activities with your child. Each time they do one successfully on their own let them colour in the relevant picture (a sock, a button, and so on). When they have coloured in all five pictures for each activity, they can colour in the children as well

Getting dressed

I can put my socks on					
I can put my shoes on the right feet					
I can put my jumper on					
I can put my coat on					
I can do up buttons					
I can do up zips					

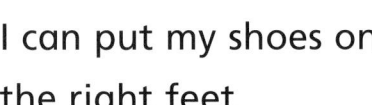

Have you ever tried organising group games at a children's party? Everyone works together towards a common goal which means there are no losers - and no tears! Here's one to try

Everyone's a winner!

Children love party games, but often get upset when their team doesn't win or when they are out. Elimination games can be great fun for children who are fast and well coordinated, but can leave some children feeling angry or disappointed. In group games everybody wins.

The feelings experienced from working together make everyone want to celebrate and this, after all, is what parties should be all about! An added advantage is that you don't end up trying to console the losers who decide they want to go home!

To play the game you need a packet of balloons and an old sheet which you don't mind cutting. If the game can be played outside so much the better, as you do need quite a large space. If not, reduce the size of the sheet and use less balloons.

The first thing you need to do is cut a hole in the centre of the sheet. Make it just large enough to pass a balloon through, then blow up all the balloons, place them on the grass or carpet and cover them with the sheet.

Organise the children so that they are standing around the four sides of the sheet. The object of the game is to move the sheet around until all the balloons have passed through the hole. Once all the balloons have been captured, everyone can enjoy a celebratory drink!

The children really enjoy working together to make this happen and hoot with laughter when any of the balloons pop, which they often do. (Do check to make sure that none of the children are frightened of balloons as some don't like loud noises.) The game can also be played with balls but it makes the sheet a lot heavier!

The chances are that you have heard your child talk about circle time. You may even have been lucky enough to join in! But what does it help them to learn?

Talking in a group

Circle time is an opportunity for children to sit together and join in activities that have been planned to give them the confidence to do exactly that - join in!

The children may be sitting in a circle (hence the name) or they may be in a smaller group with their key worker. Being in a circle is not the crucial issue. Learning to talk with friends and accept others' views is the aim of the exercise.

Many schools now have circle time and the circle time in early years settings will prepare your child for the discussion and conversation that they will encounter both at big school and in the wider community.

Stories, rhymes and the introduction of new words all form part of this special time and will encourage your child to communicate their ideas and comments. Children are encouraged to talk and to listen and will also be helped to identify their feelings about day-to-day situations and common fears.

Children usually know what they like and what they don't like! Often, however, they've made up their minds without really thinking about it. Help your child to become more aware of their own views and feelings - and be sensitive to those of others

Likes and dislikes

As they get older, it's great if children can have an open mind and be interested in trying new things. It's also good if they understand that their opinions aren't the only ones and that other people's likes and dislikes are as important as their own.

Thinking about how they've come by their own likes and dislikes can help children develop this understanding.

Look

Look at photos together of children as babies and toddlers. Talk to them about things they liked to do, say or eat that they have grown out of or don't enjoy now.

Talk

Talk to grandmas, aunties, uncles, grown-up cousins or other family and friends and find out things they didn't like when they were younger but they do like now.

Help

Help your child to draw a picture of their favourite toy and write the date on the picture. You could take a photo and date that instead. Keep the picture for a couple of months and then look at it together. Is this still their favourite toy? Can they remember what it was they liked so much about it?

21
Help your child to learn

The phrase 'equal opportunities' - and the ideas behind it - have been around for some time now. But there is still uncertainty and confusion about what it means and how we should be bringing up and educating children

Sons and daughters

Before they are born
Many parents imagine what their child will be like before it is even born. They imagine a different future for a daughter or son. For example, some fathers-to-be will dream of sharing active pursuits with a son but not with a daughter. They picture different careers and achievements. Most expectant fathers hope for a son whereas women are far less likely to express a preference.
■ What are your dreams for your child?

Babies and toddlers
Researchers have found that parents and carers of baby girls often hold them closer and cuddle them more often. Some parents talk more with baby girls. Boys are handled more energetically and encouraged to be physical earlier. This has an effect on how they learn when they're older. Boys and girls need a balance.
■ How do you play with your child?
■ How do you expect them to behave?

At school
Once at school, boys are often spoken to more than girls but in a negative way, to do with their behaviour. Girls, on the other hand, are often praised for being quiet and settled.
■ Should there be a better balance?
■ What sort of message is this sending out?

Working out who they are
Children are bombarded with all kinds of information about what it means to be a boy or a girl - from television, their friends, pictures in books, toy packaging and advertising. They are trying to work out from all these influences what being a boy or girl means to them.

As they do this, many children will behave in a stereotyped way, and say things like 'Girls can't play football' or 'Boys don't have long hair'. They are not being sexist - just trying to make sense of confusing messages.

There are many ways to be a girl or a boy and you can gently remind them that, for example, 'Some girls do play football' or 'Boys can have short or long hair'.

But they also need adults to accept their confusion and the identities they are trying out. Most of all, they need to know that we love the child and not just the 'good boy' or 'good girl'.

Communication, Language and Literacy

This area covers using language to communicate and for thinking. It relates to linking sounds and letters, early reading and sharing books and also to early writing and handwriting.

- A young child might communicate using gestures and facial expressions, for example pointing at the biscuit tin. Another or older child might say a simple phrase such as 'biscuit please'. A child who is more confident speaking may start conversations and use whole sentences, such as 'Please may I have a biscuit?'.

- Your child will enjoy sharing books with you from a very early age. Eventually they will be able to hold the book and turn the pages while you read. Later, they will know that print has meaning, start to show an interest in the words and join in with repeated words or phrases.

- At first your child will start making marks on paper which have meaning to them (but maybe not to you!). They will learn to hold a pencil and write letters, not necessarily formed correctly. By the end of their year in Reception class, most children will be able to write their name and a few simple words or short sentences such as 'I went to the shops'.

Reading to your child is one of the best ways of helping them to learn and develop

Making time to read together

Who?
Anyone can tell stories to children. You don't need any special training. You may be surprised that you enjoy it as much as your child. So why not pick up a book and start now?

When?
Choose a time of day that suits you and your child and set a routine for storytelling. Many parents choose bedtime but other times might be better for you. It could be after lunch, at bathtime or first thing in the morning. You don't need to stick to this: you can pick up a story book and read in any spare time you have during the day.

Where?
Books are easy to carry around. You can read in the bath, on the bus, up a mountain! You can read anywhere.

Why?
There are many advantages to reading and sharing stories with your child. Some of the most important reasons are:

- It will help them develop as a reader.

- They will find learning to read much easier if they know how books work: which direction to read; about covers and contents pages; what the pictures have to do with the words.

- Sharing books gives you the chance to introduce your child to a wide range of vocabulary and language.

> **What is a picture book?**
> The name 'picture book' can be confusing. A few picture books do just have pictures, but most have both words and pictures. The picture book is different from an illustrated story in that the pictures are just as important as the text in telling the story.

- Story time is an important social time. It's a chance for you to give your full attention to your child, a time of close contact and sharing.

Sharing stories with your child

Start reading to your baby as soon as you can. A new-born baby will enjoy listening to your voice. They will begin to recognise common words and language structures.

As soon they start crawling, put two or three books on a low shelf so that they can reach for them whenever they want. This means that they can start looking at books by themselves as well as sharing them with you.

Make it a rule that story time is a quiet time when all attention is focused on the book and your reading. Having the TV or radio on in the background is distracting for both of you.

From time to time, point to the words as you read. This helps your child learn where the story is coming from and what reading is all about.

As your child starts to ask questions and make comments, respond to them as much as possible. Your child learns a huge amount from talking to you and story reading can lead to some good conversations.

Young children are naturally curious and will want to ask questions about the pictures, the characters and what is happening. Help your child by encouraging them to look at the pictures and discuss what is in them rather than just listening to the words.

Wait until your child has finished looking at the picture before turning the page. Many pictures have lots of detail and the picture is every bit as important as the words.

Don't force a restless, fidgety child to listen. Try again another time. Acting out a part of the story can help the lively child to stay involved. Give them little challenges, such as 'Can you wave your trunk like the elephant in the story?'

As you get more used to reading aloud, experiment with your voice. Your child will love to hear you try out your farmyard impressions or give the characters in the story different accents!

Always aim to finish a book, even if it means leaving out chunks of the story. Children need to learn that a story has an ending. It may also help them to realise that it's worth staying around to find out how the story finishes.

Try to be patient about re-reading a book as often as your child wants it. Children learn through repetition.

Make reading a household habit. Let your child see you reading and they will model their behaviour on yours.

Tape your storytelling so you have tapes to play on car journeys or when you are busy. Your child can then listen to the tape and follow the story in the book on their own.

Let your child join in when you choose books. They will develop favourites and may enjoy the stories even more.

Use your local library. Your child will be able to join the library no matter what age they are and there will be stories to suit the interests and ability levels of all children. The librarian is a valuable source of information. Don't be afraid to ask them for advice.

Be adventurous and try new books as well as having a tried and tested repertoire. It is important to continually give children new reading experiences.

Young children like books which include collections of nursery rhymes, rhythm (Here Come the Aliens by Colin McNaughton), repetition (Not now Bernard by David McKee) and humour (The Little Princess books by Tony Ross).

Use some books with moving parts or flaps to lift. They will give your child a sense of anticipation and excitement. Try the *Spot* books by Eric Hill.

Never go anywhere without a book in your bag. A well-loved book can be handy when you need to keep your child quiet and occupied! If money is tight, scour the charity shops and car boot sales for cheap second-hand books - and take your child to the library.

What to choose

If you and your child enjoy these books, try others by the same authors - they are all well known and have written lots of excellent books for babies, toddlers and pre-school children.

For babies
All Fall Down by Helen Oxenbury (Walker)
The Baby's Catalogue by Janet and Allan Ahlberg (Puffin)
Dear Zoo by Rod Campbell (Puffin)
Maisy's Colours by Lucy Cousins (Walker)

For toddlers
Rosie's Walk by Pat Hutchins (Puffin)
The Very Hungry Caterpillar by Eric Carle (Puffin)
The Nursery Collection by Shirley Hughes (Walker)
Mr Gumpy's Outing by John Burningham (Puffin)

For young children (aged two and above)
Kipper's Birthday by Mick Inkpen (Hodder)
Elmer by David McKee (Red Fox)
Five Minutes Peace by Jill Murphy (Walker)
Katie Morag Delivers the Mail by Mairi Hedderwick (Red Fox)

The wider the range of stories children listen to and join in with, the more they will get to know how stories work. This will make it easier for them to make up their own

Understanding stories

Young children's stories will begin very simply and may well be just a slightly altered version of a story they have heard. This is a good start, so encourage your child by listening to their stories as well as telling them your own.

Try to choose lots of different kinds of stories to share. You could visit the library together to choose new ones.

As you read to your child, stop every so often and ask them what they think will happen next. Can they guess?

If your child has a favourite story, let them join in with the telling. You could start by missing off the last words of sentences and letting them say them instead. This is easier for children if the story is a rhyming one.

Look at the front cover of books with your child and try to guess what the story will be about before you read it. This will really help develop their imagination.

Choose one of their favourite stories and ask them to draw you a picture of how the story begins, what happens next and then how it ends. If they enjoy this, play with the pictures. Try muddling them up and seeing if they can put them in the right order again.

Use the pictures below to tell a well-known fairy tale - Jack and the Beanstalk. By putting the pictures in order, telling their stories and making a book, your child will learn how to describe events and about the traditions of fairy tales

Jack and the Beanstalk

What to do
- Go to the library or look on your bookshelf at home and find a book about Jack and the Beanstalk. Share the book with your child. Look carefully at the illustrations and, as you read the story, predict what might happen next.

- Look at the pictures below. What is happening in each one? Which would come first in a book?

- Colour the pictures and cut them out. Help your child to arrange them in order. Ask your child to tell you the story.

- Stick the pictures in a concertina book made from a piece of folded card. Write down the story as your child tells it.

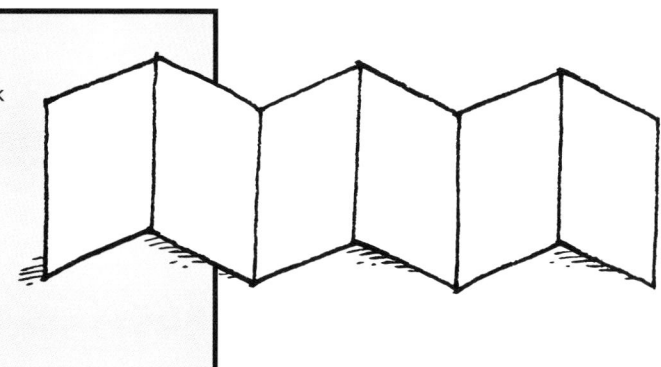

27
Help your child to learn

You can have hours of fun with nursery rhymes. They are the perfect way to develop a child's confidence in using language. Listening and responding to rhymes is one of the Early Learning Goals for Communication, Language and Literacy

Incy Wincy Spider

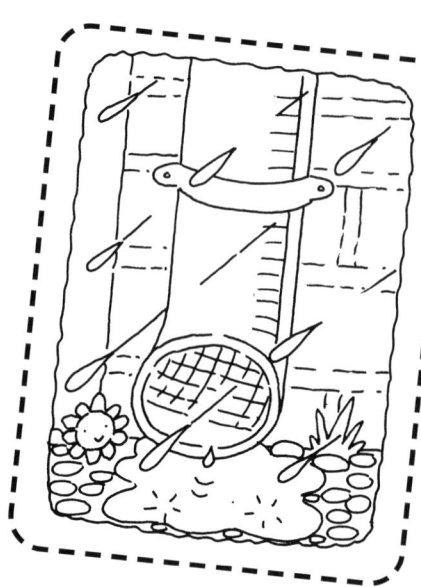

Incy Wincy Spider climbed up the water spout.

Down came the rain and washed the spider out.

Out came the sunshine, dried up all the rain,

And Incy Wincy Spider climbed up the spout again.

First cut out the pictures and stick them on to card so that they last longer. Your child can colour them in if they want. Say the rhyme together a few times and then see if your child can put the pictures in the right order.

Being able to remember the sequence of events - or words in a sentence - is an important skill in reading. Children also need to learn about the structure of stories - that they have a beginning, a middle and an end.

The cards can also be used to re-tell the rhyme as a story, adding different endings or substituting characters.

Any time is a good time to make up or tell a story. It doesn't matter who is telling the story or which story is being told; it will expand the language and stretch the imaginations of both you and your child

Telling tales

Storytelling is an enjoyable activity which strengthens the bond you have with your child. Stories seem to stay with children, often for years to come. They will learn from them without even being aware that they are learning and absorbing information.

At home, storytelling provides a unique educational opportunity very different from that of television. Whilst television entertains children's eyes and ears, storytelling entertains children's minds and imaginations. It allows children to decide and imagine what colours, sizes, shapes and sounds are in the story rather than having these elements depicted for them.

Telling stories is very different from reading books. Not having to hold a book means that you have your hands free to do actions. You can adapt it as you go along to suit your child's interest - you can even let them join in, perhaps taking it in turns to say a few words or sentences each.

It sounds daunting, but really anything goes! If you're worried about inventing a story from scratch, base it on a traditional one from memory, such as 'The three little pigs' or 'Snow White', or use familiar characters from nursery rhymes. What other adventures could Jack and Jill have? Repetition is important with very young children, so the same tale can be told over and over again.

There is no right time of day for telling stories but it's a good idea to take advantage of quiet times such as after meals, afternoon naps and bedtime when children are relaxed and receptive. It can also be used as a means of relaxing hyperactive children before bedtime or of relieving the boredom on long journeys.

Tips for the teller

To tell a story - whether it be 'The Three Little Pigs' or a short story off the top of your head - there are a few things to remember in bringing it to life.

- Your face creates the picture, so try to use as much of it as possible. Raise your eyebrows and open your eyes - or try closing one completely and squinting through the other! A moment in the mirror with an imaginary piece of toffee in your mouth will show you just how much the muscles in your face can move!

- The way we use our voice can conjure up vivid pictures in the mind of a child. It can bring a character to life and make a place feel cold, windy and wet. Experiment with:

Volume – from a whisper to a shout

Tone – from high to low

Variation – try a lisp or a stutter

- Hands, arms and shoulders can also be expressive without moving them very much. Experiment.

- Props can be helpful, too: use a puppet - something as simple as a sock with some button eyes and a tongue – soft toys or models.

On a car journey

Try playing 'I spy', then make up a story which connects the spied objects. It doesn't matter if it is nonsensical - should it bother your child they will soon let you know and suggest another word instead! These stories often produce much laughter and are brilliant for stretching the imagination.

Help your child to learn

The image of a gloomy old library with a librarian telling children to be quiet is, thankfully, a thing of the past. Today's libraries are lively welcoming places with a vast number of resources to help your child develop their reading and learning skills

Using your local library

What might you expect to find for under-fives at your local library?

- Board books for babies
- Picture books for children of all ages
- Books in a range of local community languages
- Non-fiction books to introduce new concepts in an easy to understand way
- Book lists to help you choose materials for your child
- Toys

- Library staff with a knowledge of books, reading and child development
- Computers for children to use
- Videos, audio books on tape and software for loan
- Story times and under-fives sessions
- Books and other resources on child development and health issues

Not all libraries will offer all of these facilities but why not find out what your local library provides?

Six steps to getting the best from your local library:

- Enrol your child as soon as you want to – they are never too young to join
- Take along some identification for filling in an application form
- Be adventurous and choose a mixture of picture books, stories and poetry to read aloud with your child
- Share and enjoy them with your child
- Don't worry if your child damages a book. Library staff want books to be used and are usually sympathetic to any accidental damage done
- Remember to return your books and choose some more!

There are many reasons why your child should join the local library. One major reason is that research has shown that the younger children are introduced to books the easier they will find learning to read.

Remember, your local library is:

- Fun
- Free
- A great place for children

And it will help your child develop reading and learning skills.

Join the library with your child today and help them reach their full potential.

When the shops are full of so many different books in all shapes and sizes, why go to the bother of making them? Apart from being fun, your child can learn a great deal from making books

Making books together

Making books is good because:

- It's a chance to learn a new skill.
- It's a time to work closely together.
- It helps your child learn how to have a conversation.
- It develops vital skills in many areas - maths and physical development as well as language.
- It helps your child learn how books are organised and encourages early reading.

Do this somewhere quiet!

You will need:
- some of your own simple books to compare
- A4 white paper
- safe scissors
- stapler
- drawing pencils/pens
- small photos of your child or cut-out pictures of favourite things

How to make a 4 page book all about your child.

1. fold A4
2. open out ← cut → A5
3. A5
4. Fold each in half & slot into each other.
5. staple
6. Add a title + personal picture to the front cover.
   - simple decoration
   - title: "A book about me."
   - cut out photo
   - By Jonnie — author
7. Inside - anything interesting!
   - Me and Dad.
   - I can swim.

   Writing by adult, or child's own marks + writing. Your child can tell you what to write.

Shape up!

Make a book about a favourite thing ~ in an appropriate shape.

Bath time with Nicci

Don't cut fold!

Beddy by Laura

Draw shape on the front of a 4 page book. Cut out all 4 pages together.

You may have heard the word phonics and wondered what it means. It has to do with how your child will be taught to read

Finding out about phonics

What is phonics?
Phonics describes the relationships between the sounds (called phonemes) of a language and the written symbols or letters. In English, sounds don't always match the written letters - there are at least 40 phonemes or sounds but only 26 letters! Sometimes two letters are put together to represent one sound (for example 'th').

Why is phonics necessary?
Young children do not know that spoken language is made up of words, which in turn are made up of syllables, which themselves are made up from the smallest units of sound, called phonemes. Knowing that spoken language is made up of distinct sounds is crucial for children learning to read.

Readers need a basic knowledge of phonics to make progress in reading.

But it is only one part of what children need to learn in the process of becoming literate.

Your child needs to see and hear language used in contexts which are meaningful to them - and this is where you can play a valuable role. Spending time emphasising the sounds of language will go a long way in helping your child to become a successful reader and learner. (Some suggestions for activities are given below.) Research has shown that the kind of 'coaching in context' that parents do, quite naturally, is exactly the right approach to take.

Phonemes
- Phonemes (sounds) are represented by letters.
- A phoneme can be represented by one or more letters, for example sh, ee.
- The same phoneme can be represented in more than one way, for example the ae sound in r<u>ai</u>n, s<u>ay</u> and c<u>a</u>ke.
- The same spelling may represent more than one sound, for example ie in 'f<u>ie</u>ld' and 'tr<u>ie</u>d'.

Vowel phonemes include: a (cat), e (leg), i (pig), o (dog), u (cup), ae (day), ee (feet), ie (my), oi (boy) and ear (here).

Consonant phonemes include: b (baby), d (dog), m (man), p (pen), s (sun), ch (chip, watch), sh (shop, mission).

Your child's nursery should be happy to explain the approach and system that they use, for example whether to call letters by their names (ay, bee, cee) or by their sounds (a, buh, cuh).

How you can help

- Read and re-read favourite nursery rhymes, enjoy tongue twisters and other forms of language play together.

- Re-read favourite poems, songs and stories; point out alliteration (Lauren loves lollipops!) and rhyme within them. Play around with sounds. ('I Spy', 'Make a new word' - start with 'cake', remove the letter 'c' and think about other new words like 'take', 'make', 'bake').

- Read alphabet books and make your own together.

- Talk about words. Spot words that start with the same sounds or sound patterns in the names of people, places and signs.

- Talk about letters and sounds or patterns of sound when you are writing with, for and in front of your child.

- Encourage your child in their play with magnetic, plastic or wooden letters and provide tools and materials they can use for reading and writing in their imaginary play.

- When reading together, help your child to build on what they already know and what they think the meaning is in words. Take a look at the first letter and try to work out the rest of the word (start with short consonant - vowel - consonant words, for example 'cat', not longer blends).

- You know what your child can do. You are the best judge of what they are ready to do next. The best thing you can do for your child is to help them develop a love of books and words. Through involvement in daily routines together, parents and children are naturally using the print that is all around them every day.

Your child needs to learn to recognise their name because it gives them a sense of identity. Once they start school, being able to recognise the written version of their name takes on a new meaning. They will need to find exercise books, lunchboxes, PE kits, and their own drawer or tray. Here are some ways to help

Name games

- Talk to your child about their name and the letters in it.

- Make an attractive sign together for their bedroom door, with their name as the central feature.

- Label anything which is theirs or which they use a lot, for example, a toybox, bookcase or wardrobe.

- Label your child's personal belongings clearly.

- Make a collage together of your child's name using cut-out letters from Christmas or birthday cards.

- Make letter shapes when you are playing with playdough.

- When you are out shopping, look for words which begin with the same letter as your child's name.

Remember: always begin the child's name with a capital (upper case) but make sure the rest of the letters are small (lower case).

- Make up a little story book, diary or photo album with your child's name on the front. Under each photo or picture write a sentence about what is happening, for example: Emily at the seaside. In this way you can build up a book to share together. Encourage your child to 'read' and say his or her name each time it appears in the text.

What's in a name?

At first children may see their name as a picture, remembering the shape or perhaps just the first letter. It is not unusual for children to think that the first capital (upper case) letter is the whole name. When an Emily, for example, sees a capital E, she might say 'That's me!' or 'That's Emily!'. To the child, that one letter is her name and, when writing, she will produce it over and over again. She may distinguish it from other capital letters, for example the first letters of other children's names.

A child who is beginning to discover print and who is shown alphabet letters may say 'That one's in my name'. In this way, children become ready to understand written language. Eventually they begin to realise that there is more than one element in a word. They understand that a word is made up of letters. Once they begin to discriminate between the letters, they can then develop, little by little, the idea of recognising the other letters in sequence, particularly if it is a short name.

Before encouraging children to start writing their name, always make sure they recognise it. This skill is the foundation for writing.

Through speaking and listening your child will become aware of others and develop their imagination

Learning to listen

You don't need fancy equipment to help your child become a good listener!

Play a game with bricks or even the contents of your kitchen cupboards!

- Sit together near the cupboard or brick box with a screen between you. (A chair draped with a towel works well.)

- Cue your child with one simple instruction at a time 'Put the tin of beans in front of you', then 'Place the tin of spaghetti next to the beans', and so on.

- Add instructions one by one using words such as 'in front', 'behind', 'next to' and so on.

If you put tins in place as well on your side of the screen, you can look when you finish to see if they match. Give your child time to respond and praise their efforts. Remember, they are not wrong! Don't make it a learning exercise - it's a game which should be fun!

You can take turns and let your child give you instructions. You can give an older child two or three instructions at the same time to extend their memory and concentration. As they become experienced you can introduce more words such as rectangles, cubes and cones.

- Make a simple model using bricks, Lego, or construction kits and hide it. Give the child some of the same bricks and give them instructions on how to build it. Give plenty of clues and let them make 'mistakes'. Discuss and compare the results.

- Most of all, have fun!

Use the pictures below to play a game. As your child sorts the cards according to their rhymes, they will begin to develop a sense of rhyme. The cards can also be used to improve your child's visual memory

Rhyming pairs

What to do
- Colour the pictures, cut them out and stick them onto card.
- Help your child identify all the pictures. Sort them into rhyming pairs.

- Play 'I spy a picture which rhymes with ...'.
- Lay the cards face down. In turn, pick up two. If the pictures rhyme, keep them. The winner is the one with the greatest number of pairs.

- Put out two cards which rhyme and one which does not. Ask your child to pick the odd one out.

Help your child to learn

As children become aware of words and letters they start to notice them in their environment. It is great to use this interest to help children think about why we use writing. Why not try making up your own high street?

What's in a name?

Take your child to your nearest town or row of shops and look at what shops there are. Look at the names of the shops. (Some may be jokes, like 'A cut above' or some might be people's names.)

Read the names to your child but see if they can perhaps recognise the first letter sound. At home, draw a row of shops on a long piece of paper, like a piece of old wallpaper roll. Give each shop a window and a sign.

Let your child decide what each shop will sell and draw things in the window. Then decide between you what each shop should be called and you can write the name on each sign.

Your child may not be able to read yet but they'll spot the name of their favourite fast-food restaurant and recognise the logos of well-known cars

Words and pictures

Literacy covers a whole range of skills to do with speaking, listening, reading and writing. You'll be doing a lot to help your child simply by talking to them, sharing feelings, introducing new words, asking their opinions - and listening to their response.

They may not be ready to learn to read but they will be starting to recognise that written words mean something. Take every opportunity to use the everyday environment and develop their awareness of literacy around them.

Look for lots of signs and words. Talk about what they mean and how sometimes people write words and sometimes they draw pictures. Here are some ideas for things to spot when you're out together.

You can also look for street names, shop names, notices at the bus or railway station, road signs or maps on the motorway.

Look at the sounds the words begin with and encourage your child to listen for them. Play fun games to rhyme words with the words they have read.

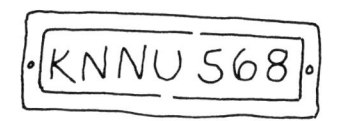

Number plates Car logos, Names of cars

Street signs Talk about what they may be saying.

Words on vehicles

Signs in public places

Most children don't need any encouragement to talk - to you, to each other and even to themselves! - but you can help them to develop their language by making them think about the words they use and by introducing new words

Time for talk

Being able to see similarities and differences between things is a vital skill for young children as it provides a foundation for learning to read and write. Here are some ideas for games to play which will help them develop that skill.

Encourage your child to look at things really carefully, to listen to what you say and to talk about what they see and learn new words.

Looking at passports
Let your child have a look at your passport and those of any other family members. Explain that the photograph in our passport as well as the description tells people who we are. In every passport we need our name, place and date of birth, a photograph, signature and any distinguishing marks we may have. These details tell the people checking passports who we are and they can tell by looking at the photograph if the picture is of us. People are similar and different in various ways and this must be emphasised. We are all similar in that we have a face yet our features make us different from each other. Can your child make their own passport?

People puzzles
Cut out some pictures of people from old clothing catalogues or magazines. The sizes of the people must be in proportion, for example a picture of a child must not be larger than one of an adult.
(You could use photographs of people in your family or friends, if you have any that you don't mind cutting up.)

Stick the pictures onto cardboard and cut them into two or three sections. Put a set of, say, two or three pictures in a box, then ask your child to put them back together. (Too many sets at first may confuse them - you can give them more once they get the hang of it.) While they try to work it out, talk about what they are doing. Whose head do you think this belongs to? Do you think these legs belong to a man or a woman? Which one's got the red jumper? When the pictures are finished, talk about what the people look like - the colour of their hair, eyes, clothes, their size, and so on. How are they the same? How are they different? Compare the heights of the people and see if your child can put them in order from the biggest to smallest or smallest to biggest. This is an excellent way to help children see similarities and differences between people.

Help your child to learn

You are your child's first and most important teacher.
You can help your child develop as a writer at home

The first stages of writing

The development of writing

1. Drawing
2. Scribbling
   - random
   - controlled
3. Letter-like forms
4. Letters
   - random
   - patterned
5. Invented spelling
6. Conventional writing ages

Ages 2 – 3yrs

Ages 8 – 9yrs

1998 High/Scope Educational Research Foundation

How to help your child develop as a writer:

- Talk to your child when you are writing. Children need many opportunities to watch and talk to adults who are writing, so that they can understand why people write, what writing looks like and what happens to writing.

- Give your child a chance to get involved in day-to-day writing. Let your child see you writing and be with you when you are writing; this might be writing shopping lists, an added line and kisses at the end of letters, birthday cards, invitations or phone messages.

- Give your child freedom to scribble and experiment with a wide variety of paper, thick and thin crayons, pencils and felt pens.

- Very young children will grasp a pencil with their whole hand (like holding a dagger) and will then move on to holding the pencil in a more usual way. Show your child how to hold a pencil and help them towards holding the pencil in a normal way, but do not force them to do it.

- Young children may not have decided which hand they like to write with and may swap from left to right for some time. Eventually they will show a preference for one hand and use it consistently.

- Let your child talk to you about their writing. Who is the writing for? If it is a story, ask questions: 'Who is in it?' 'What will happen next?' 'How will it end?'

- Sometimes you could write for your child. Let your child dictate stories, letters, lists, cards.

- Why not give your child a scrapbook so that they can save examples of their writing and drawing. You and your child might like to look back at these and talk about them together. The scrapbook will provide an interesting record of the development of your child's understanding of writing.

- Show your child that you value their writing. Put it on the wall, as you would do a painting.

- Praise and value all their writing and don't expect their writing to look like adult writing. Don't take over! Let them experiment. This is a stage of development - don't rush things.

- Let your child play with writing toys, for example magnetic letters, magic slate, printing sets, blackboard and chalk, Post Office sets.

- Remember! The secret to raising a life-long reader and writer is to read and write with them, with pleasure not pressure!

Make your own postcard like the one below and let your child have fun writing to a friend, real or imaginary. They can draw and colour their own picture on the back

'I can write like mummy'

Your child's first awareness of writing will come from watching you and other adults writing as you do your day-to-day activities, such as filling in forms, signing cheques and writing letters. Children are fascinated by it and soon want to mimic the same actions. This is an important stage in their development and should be encouraged as it is the start of their journey to becoming a writer.

At first their writing will be squiggles as this is how they see your writing. Gradually, with encouragement and praise, it will become more sophisticated and include symbols such as shapes, letters and numbers.

As they learn to spell their name, this and the letters in it will be included everywhere. Once your child has started school and begins to learn the alphabet and the sounds those letters make, they will be able to start writing simple words.

You want your child to want to write and to enjoy learning to write, so be positive with whatever they produce - there is nothing more off-putting than the thought that you will always get it wrong.

Encourage your child to try writing in all situations - when they are playing, writing shopping lists, birthday cards, filling in blank forms, recipes - anything!

Try to have suitable materials available for your child to use whenever they need them, be ready to answer their questions and show by example, for instance bring their attention to what you are writing and why.

Useful materials

Pens
Paper (of all sizes)
Note books
Pencils
Old diaries
Scissors
Rubbers
Ruler
Hole punch
Folders
Blank forms (from the bank or post office)
Envelopes
Pencil sharpener
Sticky paper

Did you make a scrap book when you were young? Scrap books are quite cheap to buy or you can fold up some sheets of paper to make your own. They are a good way to encourage your child to start writing

Making a scrap book

Children can cut and stick anything into a scrap book, but there's lots of learning to be had as you talk together about the pictures, help children use scissors and glue and encourage them to write.

What can you do?
Sort out old birthday, Christmas or other celebration cards, used stamps, comics, magazines or catalogues, postcards or even old or duplicate photos.

Ask your child what they would like to put in their scrap book. Perhaps they'd like to make up a story or an art show using old cards? Maybe they want to make a dinosaur or favourite character book or even a book about themselves? Of course, they may just want to cut and stick their favourite pictures into the book.

Whatever they choose, remember to ask them about each page. Encourage them to write a heading or a caption for each page. If they like to make up their own writing then great, but perhaps they might like you to help them by writing words for them to copy or doing some of the pages for them. Writing can be quite exhausting for young children!

Tip
Although it's a bit messier than stick glue, try to use white glue because it works a lot better.

Don't feel you have to rush to finish making the book. The great thing about scrap books is that they can be added to over months. Try to remember when you go out visiting, or away on holiday, to encourage children to collect souvenirs for their scrapbook. Then back at home they can stick tickets and leaflets, stamps and even foreign coins into their book and write their best memories of their time away.

It's easy to do far too much for children. If you want them to grow up able to think things through and solve problems, then you need to encourage them to do just that. Here are some simple things you can do to get your child thinking

Help your child to think

Talk about everything!
Talk as you do things together - going for a walk, laying the table, buying the groceries, looking for special cars, the change of seasons, buying a present.

Notice everything around you!
Discuss colours, shapes, sizes, smells, sounds, tastes, textures, materials.

Compare everything!
Is it bigger, smaller, wider, narrower, fatter, thinner, heavier, lighter?

Use the question words!
When? How? What? Where? Why?

Try to use the phrase: Stop! Let me think!

Collect a treasure box!
Gather for making and painting - shiny paper, coloured bits and pieces, small and big boxes, stickers and ribbons, buttons and bows, interesting rubbish.

Essential words
What do you think? What would you do? How could we --- ? Is there a better way? How could we change this? What would happen if?

It's not a question of money! The most precious gift is time and talk!

Measure everything!
How long? How wide? How thick? How tall? How deep?

Count everything!
Tins in cupboards, packets on shelves, biscuits for tea, chips, knives and forks, socks out to dry.

Have a dressing-up box!
Pretend, imagine, invent, create, re-design, re-build.

Say where everything is!
Behind, in front, upside down, back to front, on the top, underneath.

Praise them when they do well!
Have sticker stars, points for good behaviour, red and green lights or flags for 'Stop!' and 'Go!'

Show how things are done!
Take things to pieces, build them again, cook together, paint together, clean together.

Fair discipline
Agree ground rules, discuss problems, talk things through, don't be afraid to use fair sanctions.

Mathematical Development

Mathematics in the early years is about encouraging children to use numbers - as labels, for counting and calculating. Children should be helped to develop mathematical language, such as 'bigger' or 'smaller ' when talking about shapes or comparing quantities.

- Your child will enjoy number rhymes and songs from an early age. Later on they will say number names and try to count but may not have the order right or miss numbers out. You may hear 'one, two, three, four, five, six, eight, ten'. By the time they leave Reception class most children will be able to count reliably up to ten everyday objects and say and use number names in order in familiar contexts, for example, counting the candles on their birthday cake or recognising the number on their front door.

- At first your child will enjoy playing with shapes, for example in a shape sorter. When they are older they will be able to talk about shapes of everyday objects, for example for a biscuit they may say 'That's a circle', for a sandwich 'That's a triangle'.

- Young children enjoy threading beads and finger painting and may make random patterns. They will move on to copying and carrying on a pattern, for example 'Red, blue, red, blue - What comes next? Yes, red'. Older children will make more complicated patterns and recognise patterns in numbers.

You can help your child with maths not only by teaching them how to count but by using words to do with size, comparing and measuring

What we mean by number

Numbers are part of everyday language and not just something we use for counting. If you want to be able to help your child grasp this in their important early years it is vital to understand this point.

It is perfectly possible for a child of four to be able to read and to count up to a hundred. What might be overlooked is that at this stage the child will have no more understanding of the words than the numbers. They simply do not know what they mean until they come within their experience.

Numbers are an abstract idea. Two cannot exist by itself, there has to be two of something. This makes it more difficult for a child to come to terms with. It is important for you to help your child here by teaching not only counting skills (blowing dandelions, finger rhymes, repetitive songs) but also by introducing your child to mathematical language. The sooner your child understands this language the easier it will be for them to work with numbers in the future.

Mathematical language is words like big, small, high, low, thick, thin, high, higher, highest. These are everyday words and the reason why they are classed as mathematical is that they all involve some form of measurement or comparison.

The best help you can give your child is to use these words whenever the opportunity presents itself. It is surprising how often this will happen. Setting the table, for instance, can give an opportunity for counting and comparison to make sure that everyone has an appropriate place setting. These practical activities let your child make the necessary connections between numbers in the abstract and their everyday use.

You are in the best possible position to take advantage of these natural learning opportunities and to use mathematical terms and practical examples, so that your child becomes confident with them.

Children need to have practical mathematical experiences before they can understand what is really meant by three cups or five pencils. This is not as difficult as it sounds. Your everyday routines at home provides a variety of situations in which to explore numbers with your child

Counting at home

Meal times

Why not set the table together, asking questions as you go along? 'Who will be here for tea today?' 'How many spoons will we need?' Count out the spoons together as your child puts them on the table and repeat the sequence until the table is set.

Spot the number

When you're out for a walk or on a trip to town, play 'Spot the numbers' on buses, houses, cars and displays. You can also play this game at home, finding numbers on remote control panels, telephones and clocks.

In the kitchen

Do some baking together, choosing a recipe from a book and reading the amounts for each ingredient as you go along. Look for numbers in recipes and on the scales. Ask your child to count as they transfer spoons of flour from scales to bowl.

Counting games

Have fun sorting small objects such as buttons, shells and conkers into sets using empty margarine tubs and counting the contents of the tubs. Vary the game by writing the numbers one to five on pieces of paper and put a piece in each tub. Count the correct number of objects into each tub. You can play this game with bigger boxes and toys as a way to encourage tidying up!

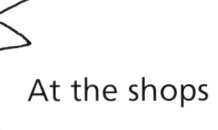

Buy one, get one free!

At the shops

Ask questions as you go around the supermarket. 'Can you put four pots of yoghurt into the trolley?', 'We've got one box of cereal at home, can you choose two more?' Back at home sort the shopping into sets of tins, packets, boxes and plastic bottles and count the groups you have made.

By making learning about numbers a fun experience you can be sure your child will be counting with greater understanding.

Make a fun number line frieze with your child, one which they will love to have on their wall

Make your own number frieze

You will need:
- 10 pieces of card
- paint or thick markers
- scissors
- glue
- sticky tape
- magazines, catalogues or wrapping paper featuring their favourite characters or things which interest them (for example, Bob the Builder, animals, dinosaurs)

What to do:
Help your child to paint one large number on each piece of card, starting at one through to ten.

When they are dry, take each number and find the appropriate number of objects or images on the wrapping paper. For example, one Bob, two cats, three hard hats, and so on.

Help your child to cut them out and glue them on the correct piece of card.

Tape the cards together in the right sequence.

The frieze is now ready to put up!

You can ask your child questions about their number line, for example:
How many ....?
Are there more ..... or .....?
There are six somethings on the line, can you tell me what they are?
Which number comes after three?

Which number comes after three?

Learning to count and getting the number names in the right order needs plenty of practice, but should also be enjoyable

Rhymes and stories

Nursery rhymes and poems are an excellent way to help your child learn to count. Many rhymes mention number, for example:

'One, two, three, four, five';
'One, two, buckle my shoe';
'Five little ducks went swimming one day';
'Five little speckled frogs'.
Not only do these rhymes encourage counting, but when the children are listening to, saying or singing them, they are experiencing the rhythm and pattern of the words. Pattern is extremely important in developing mathematical thinking.

Using old magazines
Don't throw out old magazines and colour supplements. Have some fun with them! Go through them with your child. You will find a wealth of brightly coloured pictures to encourage counting.

Cut them out and mount them on a large piece of paper or in a scrap book. Write the correct number with a felt pen, next to each picture. You will then have an attractive, cheap, mathematical game that you can look at again and again.

One, two, three, four, five

Once I caught a fish alive.

Six, seven, eight, nine, ten

Then I let it go again.

Why did you let it go?

Because it bit my finger so.

Which finger did it bite?

This little finger on my right!

Playing games with dice or cards is an enjoyable way of helping children to count and recognise the numbers one to ten. There are many good games to buy but, if you take an ordinary pack of cards, you can make up your own, which will help your child's understanding of numbers

Play your cards right!

Making twins

Remove the kings, queens, and jacks from a pack of cards. Shuffle and deal six cards to each player. Put the rest in a pile, face down on the table.

The first person takes the top card from the pile. They look at their seven cards to see if they have a twin (two of the same number). If they do, they put them face up in front of themselves and then choose one of their remaining cards to throw away, putting it face up next to the pile. If they cannot make a twin, they still have to throw away a card.

The next player can choose to pick up either the top card thrown away or one from the pile, to see if they can make a twin.

Players can only put down one twin at a time, when it is their turn. The first to make three twins is the winner.

> **What this helps children learn**
> Learning to recognise numbers and to count in a variety of play situations helps children to develop an understanding of number values and a growing confidence. This will stand them in good stead when they come to learn mathematical skills in more formal situations.

Don't throw away those old egg boxes - they can be used to make a valuable mathematical toy!

Trucks and trains

Using one closed egg box with a cardboard tube stuck in it to make a funnel, and several open egg boxes tied on behind, you can make a train whose journey around the house will create fun and games and encourage your child to count to ten and recognise the numbers one to ten.

- Using small toys as passengers, place some in each truck and encourage your child to count how many there are altogether.

- Let your child put some toys in the truck and count them. (Always encourage your child to touch each toy as they count.)

- Move on to talking about which truck has the most/least toys. How many more should we put in this truck to fill it up?

- Write out the numbers one to ten on cards. As your child counts the toys in each truck, they can begin to select the correct number card to go in each truck.

This letter posting and sorting activity will help your child to recognise and match numbers. You might like to talk about who has the most/least letters and the details on the collection panel on the post box

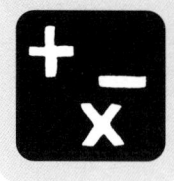

Letter-box game

Make a post box out of an old cardboard box, like the one shown, and address some cards or envelopes to real or imaginary friends.

Play at posting the letters in the box. Empty the box then sort and count letters.

- How many letters are for Sam?
- How many are for Amy?
- Who has the most?
- How many letters are for Dale Road?
- What time is the next collection?

Collection Times
1
10 a.m.
1 p.m.
4 p.m.

Amy
3, My street

Sam
3, My street

Ben
1, The Walk

Joe
7, Dale Road

Lily
1, The Walk

Sam
3, My street

David
4, Pen Street

Help your child to learn

There are lots of games you can play outside which will develop your child's understanding of number, shape and measurement, and encourage them to use mathematical language. Here's one to try which you can then adapt and use over and over again

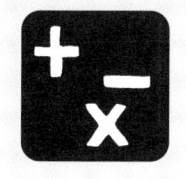

A mathematical treasure hunt

Talk to your child about going on a treasure hunt in the garden or the local park. What do they think they might find? Make a list of things to find using numbers, words and pictures. We have given you one to try but you might want to make your own.

During the hunt, help your child to find as many of the items on the list as possible. Some items, such as flowers, you can spot and count but not actually pick. Encourage them to look carefully and count independently so they feel a strong sense of achievement.

There may also be opportunities to ask questions that will develop your child's use of mathematical language. Try some of these:

- How many steps do you think it will take to reach the gate? Guess! Were you right?

- How many birds can you see in that tree? Are there more birds in that tree over there?

- Which is the tallest tree you can see?

- What can you see in front of the wall?

- If I pick up one more stick, how many will we have?

- Oh dear, I've dropped one of the leaves! How many have we got left?

- Which of us can run the fastest? (You are allowed to cheat and let them win!)

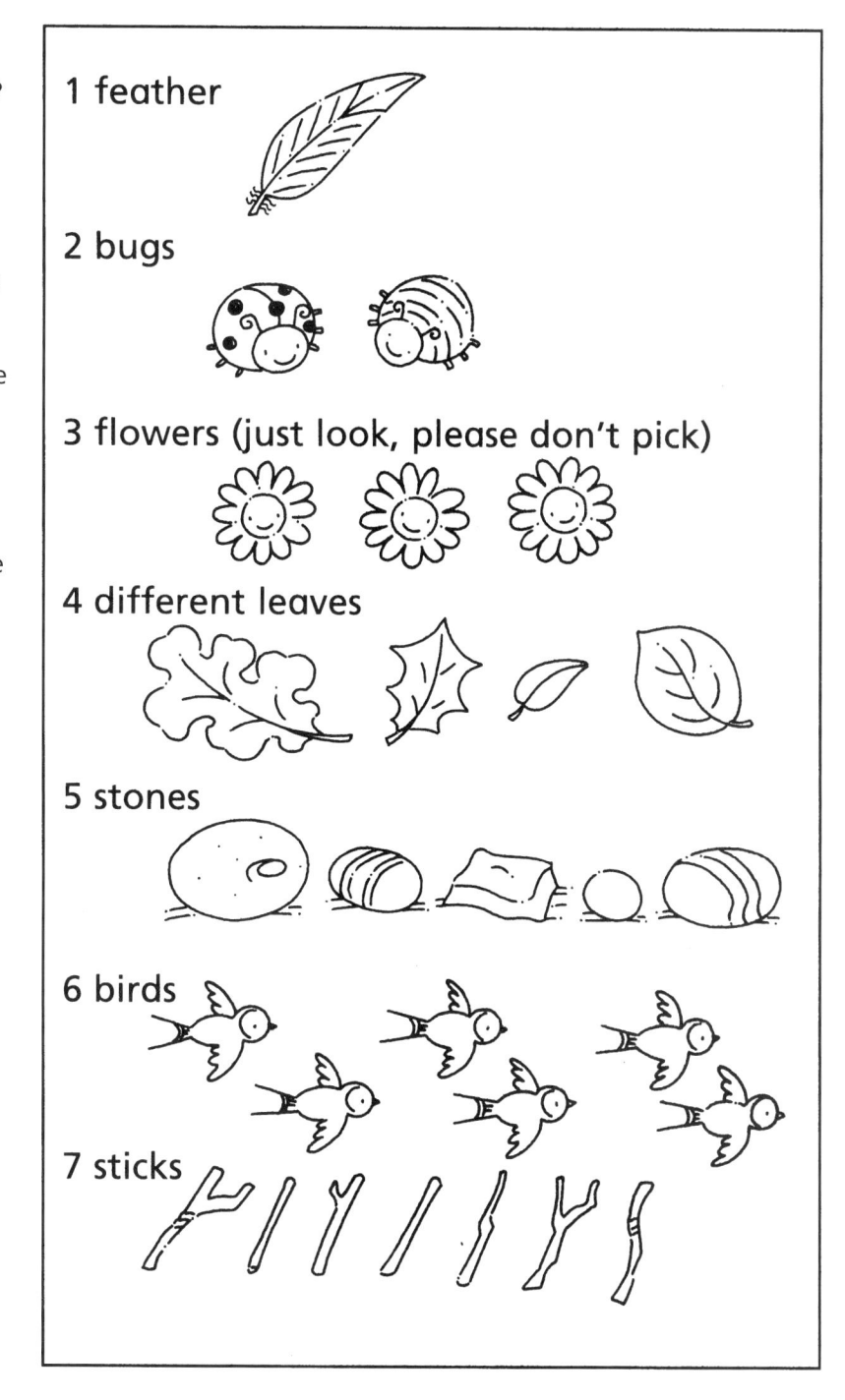

1 feather

2 bugs

3 flowers (just look, please don't pick)

4 different leaves

5 stones

6 birds

7 sticks

Help your child to learn

Sorting is something that your child is encouraged to do a lot at pre-school or school. But why is it so important and what can you do at home to help?

What is sorting?

Sorting the magazine rack (type)
All comics/non-comics

Sorting the washing (colour)
Plain white/not plain white

We all sort things every day without realising that sorting is what we are doing. We sort out crockery into plates, cups, bowls, we sort our clothes and some people sort their CDs or tapes! All this sorting is to make our lives easier to manage and means that we can make better use of the time available.

Children need to be taught the different ways of sorting. As they get older they will start to classify objects naturally (things that taste nice and things that don't) but may not at this stage be able to say why they group things in particular ways. To be able to use sorting as a useful tool later in life, children need to learn how to improve their ability. At nursery or pre-school, children are mainly encouraged to sort according to colour, shape, size and type. At home this can be reinforced in many everyday situations.

Sorting is always based on comparison of attributes – matching like with like. It is a good idea to start off using a positive and negative, for example, all plain white/not plain white. Using the terms plain white/patterned might confuse children as there may be some objects that are neither plain nor patterned, but another plain colour.

Sorting the clean washing (size)
All adult clothes/clothes that are not adult. Children who manage this easily could go on to sort their own clothes, mum's clothes, dad's clothes, baby sister's clothes etc.

Sorting the shopping (shape)
All the cylindrical items/all non-cylindrical items

Help your child to learn

This activity will encourage your child to look closely, to learn new words such as 'match' or 'pattern'. It will also help them to learn that some things are the 'same' and some are 'different'

Sort the socks!

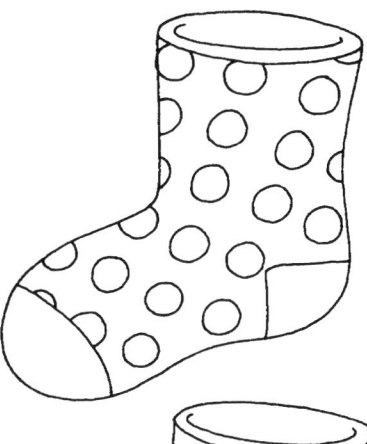

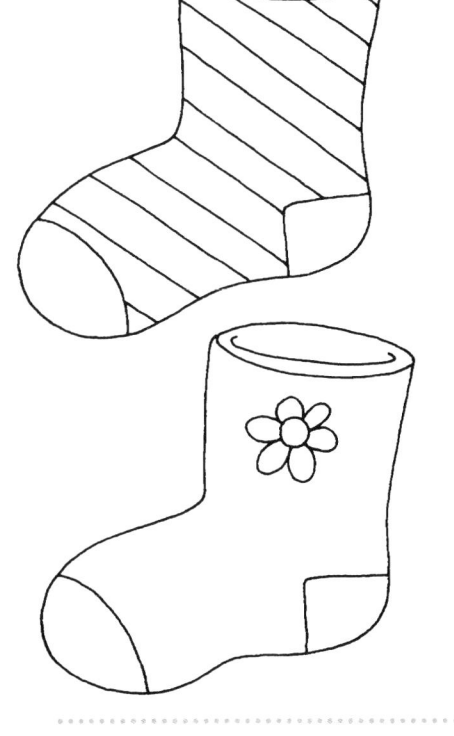

- See if your child can draw a line to join the socks that have the same pattern. You can talk about the kinds of patterns that are on the socks (spots, stripes, crosses) or whether they are plain.

- Let them colour the socks which they have joined so that they are the same. Do they know the names of all the different colours?

- Can they say how the socks are the same? They will be the same in three ways (pattern, colour and size). If they do not come up with size straightaway you may need to give them a bit of help.

Here's an idea for a game which develops children's mathematical skills but at the same time is so much fun it could even be played at a birthday party!

Going on a bear trail

Draw some bears on a sheet of paper, making each one slightly different. This is the master sheet. Your child can colour them if they want. Copy them on to another piece of paper - colour them the same to match - and this time cut them out. Stick each bear on to a piece of card and cover with sticky backed plastic. Punch a hole in the top and thread a loop of string through the hole to make the card easy to hang up.

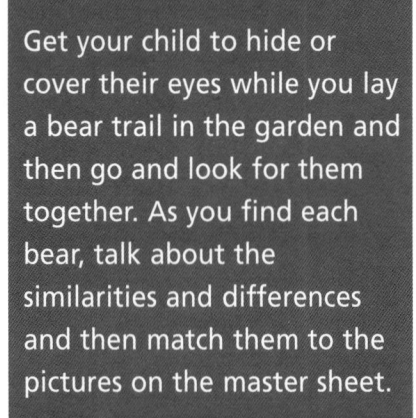

Get your child to hide or cover their eyes while you lay a bear trail in the garden and then go and look for them together. As you find each bear, talk about the similarities and differences and then match them to the pictures on the master sheet.

If you're not artistic, you can use the bears on this page, or cut identical pictures from magazines and use them in the same way instead of drawing pictures.

You can help teach your child the language of maths in everyday situations

You've grown!

As children grow and need new clothes, it is an excellent chance to talk about size - length, height and width.

- Oh dear! Those jeans are too 'short' for you now. Your legs have grown too 'long'.

- This anorak is far too 'short'. It won't keep you warm enough. You have grown much 'taller'.

- Look how much 'bigger' this new jumper is. The sleeves are 'longer' than your old one and it is 'wider' across the shoulders. You are growing 'tall'!

- Can you reach your book off the shelf? Well done! You are certainly 'taller'. You couldn't do that last year.

Bring out some of their baby clothes and compare the sizes. Measure their clothes against those of older/younger brothers and sisters.

My legs are too long!

Mummy's jumper's too big!

Words to do with size include:

big/tall/small
bigger than/taller than/smaller than
long/short
longer than/shorter than

You can help develop mathematical thinking and vocabulary by talking to your child and asking questions in everyday situations

Making maths fun

To understand the concepts of length, width and capacity, children need to hear you use words such as 'longer than,' 'shorter than', 'empty' and 'full' in meaningful situations.

In the bath, at the kitchen sink or in the paddling pool, let your child play in the water with containers of various shapes and sizes.

Provide a plastic teapot or jug for pouring and encourage emptying and filling.

Ask questions such as:
Which one do you think holds the most water?

Is the pot nearly full?

What do you think is happening to the water? Where is it going?

■ Help them pour their own drinks from a jug.

■ Allow them to 'help' washing up.

■ Dry sand play provides similar opportunities.

Sorting and counting clothes pegs of differing colours and shapes helps children's knowledge of number

Washing day maths

Let your child simply play with and sort the pegs in your basket.

- How many red pegs are there?
- Can you find more pegs this shape? How many?
- Are there more green pegs than yellow ones?
- If I take two of these, how many will you have left?

When pegging out clothes, talk about how many pegs you need.

- I think I need three pegs for this big towel. Can you give me three please?
- Do you think I need three for this towel? No - it is smaller, two will do.

Recognising pattern is an important mathematical skill. A basket full of socks provides a good opportunity to develop understanding of this.

- Let's peg all the socks in pairs. Can you find the one which matches this?

When they are all pegged on the line, it is easy to compare length and size - longer/shorter than, larger/smaller than.

When everything is pegged out, count how many items there are or discuss which is the largest/smallest.
- Are there more socks than hankies?

Now go in for a drink and a cuddle and read *Mrs Mopple's Washing Line* by Anita Hewett (published by Picture Puffin) and hope it doesn't rain!

Cooking is one of many activities you can share with your child at home which can be a real learning experience

Maths in the kitchen

Let your child help out when you are weighing things for baking cakes or cooking dinner. By letting them help out and by talking to them and asking questions as you weigh out ingredients, you can help them develop basic mathematical thinking and vocabulary.

Using the language of comparison - heavier than, lighter than - in meaningful situations, introduces and reinforces important mathematical concepts.

- Let them see the pointer move as they put more on the scales.

- Use words like weigh, heavy, heavier than, light, lighter than.

- When you're in your local supermarket or shop, watch when things, such as fruit, vegetables, cheese or meat, are being weighed out.

- Play shops together using the scales to weigh fruit or vegetables.

By hearing you use the language, your child will become familiar with the concepts of heavy, heavier, heaviest and light, lighter, lightest and gradually become confident in using the words themselves.

How often does tidying up become a battleground? Toys are all over the floor, you're tired, and your child won't co-operate! But make it into a game and the toys could be back in the box in no time at all!

It's time to tidy up!

These questions should get your child using and thinking about mathematical language as you tidy up. Children's mathematical ideas develop alongside a growing awareness of language. Each selection of toys presents a different challenge.

- 'Can you find four bricks to put into your toy box?'

- 'I bet I can find three Action Men before you find two Teddies.'

- 'How many pieces of jigsaw can you pick up? Have you got more than I have?'

- 'I can see a car under the table. Who'll get it first?'

- 'How many red toys can you put into the box?'

- 'Which toy is nearest to the TV/ the table/ the door? Good, put it in the box.'

A word of warning, however - don't make it too much fun or your child might want to tip them all out and start the game again!

Position

up/down	in front/behind
above/on top	inside/outside
over/under/below	through
top/bottom	next/beside
before/after	opposite
between	

Numbers one to ten

How many ...?

Comparison

more/less	more than/less than
same number	greater/smaller
heavier/lighter	longer/shorter
taller/shorter	higher/lower

Help your child to learn

Young children need lots of experience in using the mathematical language of time and help understanding about the passing of time before they can even begin to learn to tell the time by looking at a clock

The language of time

When young children ask 'Is it time for my programme?' they don't mean 'Is it 3.15?' but 'Is it the time in my day when I watch TV?'

The question gives you the chance to help your child understand the language of time.

'No, it's too early. You can watch after lunch.'

'You must put away your toys before watching TV.'

'You only watch TV in the morning.'

'You can watch this afternoon.'

Children begin to appreciate the passing of time by relating it to their own interests.

'Before you have a biscuit you must wash your hands.'

'Later on you can have a story.'

Using important family events will help your child understand the passing of the days, weeks, or months.

Make a weekly chart using pictures to pick out an important daily event. A monthly chart is also helpful, showing family birthdays, holidays and so on.

Your child will then begin to understand the order of days, months, and the passing of time.

Words to do with time:
yesterday
today
tomorrow
morning
afternoon
night
week
weekend
before
after
soon
now
later
earlier
takes longer
takes less time

Monday	Tuesday	Wednesday	Thur
I go to the park.	Grandma comes.	I go swimming.	Mu

Young children spend a lot of time and energy exploring space and movement. These explorations are a sound foundation for later thinking, especially relating to maths

Exploring space and movement

Children use their whole bodies at first, for example, going up steps and down slides, through tunnels and into dens or cupboards. As these movements become more skilled, they post things through letter boxes, put things into bags and place pieces into jigsaw puzzles.

Through their many explorations, children learn to work out what will fit in or through a space.

Eventually, they can estimate by looking at an object, for example whether it will fit into a container.

> William (aged four) drew a picture for his mum. He wanted to put it into an envelope. I held the envelope open for him. He struggled to put his picture in and it jutted out when he had done it. He wanted to seal the envelope so I suggested folding his picture. He said, 'I know – I'll cut the edge off and then it'll fit'. And it did.

Children explore with their whole bodies and also manipulate a variety of small objects. These explorations are the foundation for later thinking. If children have opportunities to use their whole bodies fully and freely for as long as possible and also to handle small objects in their own ways, then they have a sound foundation for all curriculum areas, particularly maths.

> Natasha played with blocks often at nursery. At home she liked pretending to iron and would fold the clothes precisely. She was particularly interested in symmetry. At school she is forging ahead with maths.

Young children will use anything that is around to:

- line up
- carry around
- scatter
- cover
- make circles

and a number of other patterns. These patterns are not neat and tidy but children use them to make discoveries about the world, so they are important.

You can help your child by giving them the chance to climb, ride, move and build things. Visits to the park or soft play areas are helpful. Riding bikes, scooters or tractors help children to become skilled in moving at speed, changing direction and judging distance.

We sometimes cringe when we see young children swinging a sword or spade around, but they are learning how far away from other people they need to be to not hit them. Helping children to make paper swords makes sure that they can play these games safely.

We do not always recognise how much children know about the hobbies we have. If you are a tennis player or a golfer, the chances are that your child would like to have a go. A plastic golf set or rackets and balls help children with hand-eye co-ordination.

Quantities of objects, for example, corks, lids, pegs and buttons, offer children an opportunity to manipulate these items in different ways. They might line them up or wrap them up, solving problems like how big a piece of paper they need to cover objects. String, sticky tape and tape measures all help with learning about length.

Children will use whatever is around, for example, cushions or video cases. It is not always easy to appreciate how important these explorations are to your child. If you can be convinced that they may well help them with advanced level maths, you will probably be a lot more tolerant!

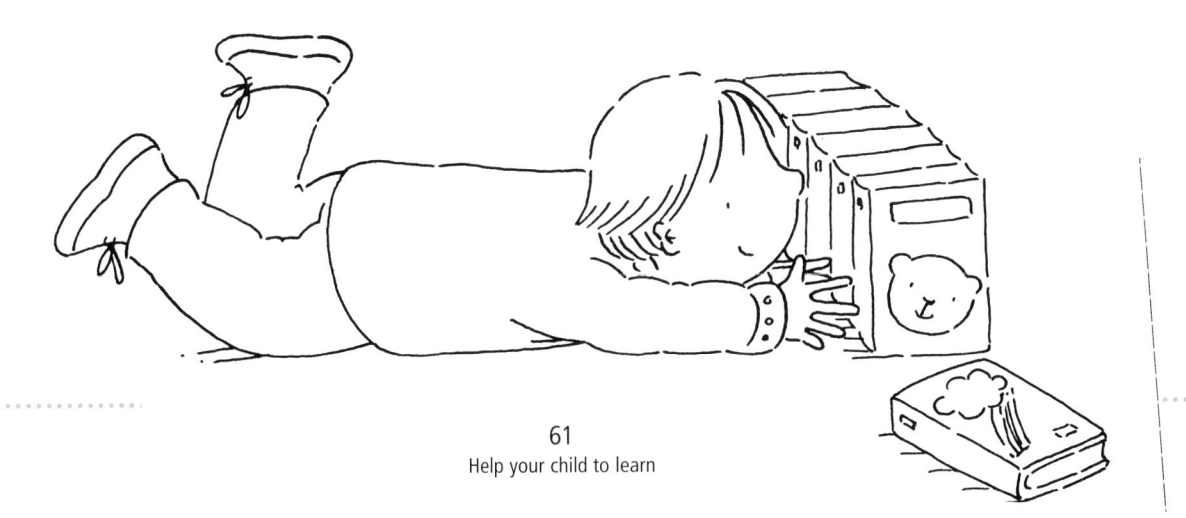

Do you remember going to the shop when you were little, clutching a few coins to buy sweets? Today, young children don't have as many opportunities to handle coins for themselves, so we need to come up with simple activities using money. Learning to use coins and to give change is too complicated for young children but they can begin to learn the names of the coins

Sam the very silly snake

Empty some coins out of your purse or pocket (1p, 2p, 5p, 10p, 20p, 50p, £1). Let your child sort the coins into the different types. You want them to look carefully at the coins - at their colour ('Let's find all the silver ones') and at their shape (putting together all the 50p pieces).

Now use some of these 1p, 2p, 5p, 10p, 20p and 50p coins for the fun activity about Sam the Snake.

Sam the very silly snake
Sam the snake is a very silly snake. He has swallowed some coins and is poorly. Let's see which coins he has swallowed.

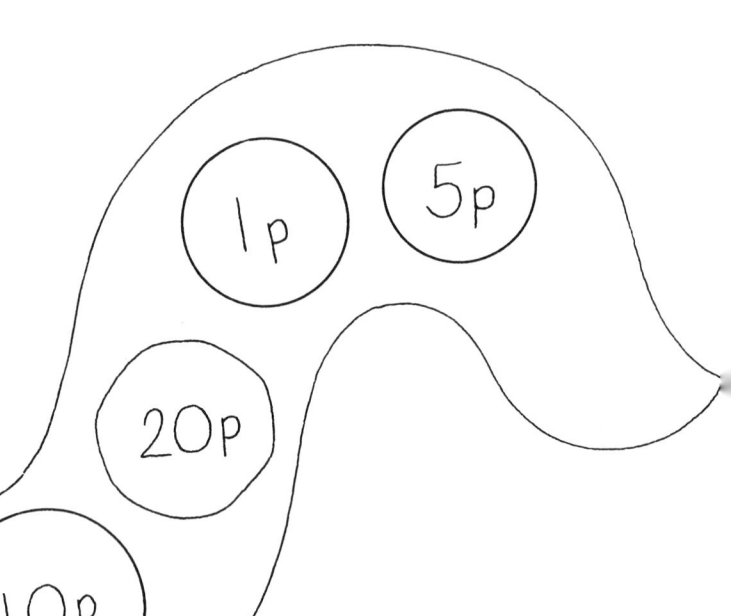

Begin with the smallest size and put a coin into the matching shape. Name each coin (for example, 'a two pence') as it is put on the snake. If there is an empty space, you might say, 'Sam the Snake must not have swallowed ... a 20 pence today'. If there are two (or more) of the same coin then these can be placed on top of each other.

When all the coins are in place, help your child to name the coins.

Goodness me! Sam the snake has swallowed ... a ten pence, a two pence, another two pence, and so on .... 'What a lot of coins he swallowed today! No wonder Sam the snake felt so poorly with all those coins inside him. What a very silly snake!'

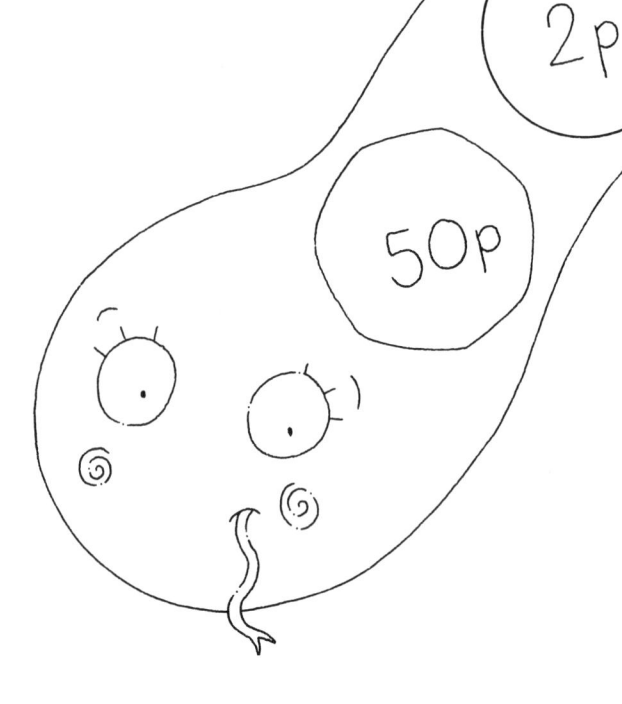

Here are some ideas of how you can help your child to understand and name shapes

Learning about shape

Using old birthday/Christmas cards, cut out some circles, squares, triangles and rectangles in different sizes. You can make all sorts of pictures together, either on the floor as a game to play over again or glue them onto backing paper.

You can use the same ideas to draw large pictures for your child to colour - they could colour the triangles red, the circles yellow, and so on.

If you are going out to the park, shopping, or visiting friends then look for shapes. Play a game on the way, finding shapes - a square paving slab, a triangle at the end of a roof, rectangular doors.

Play I-spy using shapes rather than letter sounds. You can do this at any time whether bath time, bed time or just cup of tea time.

Use food for shape naming - what shape is a fish finger, a biscuit or a spaghetti hoop? Perhaps they could choose what shape the sandwiches are for lunch or help cut circles from left-over pastry.

> Children learn more from their parents than anyone else. Learning is a part of growing up, a social experience that requires your involvement. You don't need much equipment or materials, but short spans of time spent with you can, and does, achieve a lot.

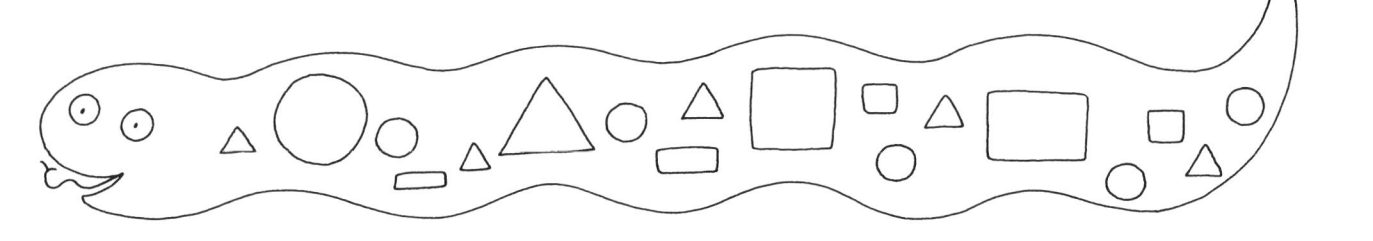

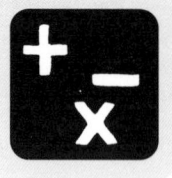

Exploring shapes that fit together helps children to learn about two-dimensional shapes. It's a really fun way of doing maths!

Patterns with shapes

Talk to your child about shapes that fit together (this is called tessellating). Go for a walk and see if you can find any examples. Rectangular slabs fit together to make pavements. Square tiles fit together in the bathroom or kitchen.

Show them the square tiles below which fit together - or you could draw your own on a sheet of paper. Help your child to decorate the tiles how they like. What about colouring them in a repeating pattern such as blue, red, blue, red, or they could do a zigzag design.

Let your child cut out the tiles and stick them back together on a piece of card. They could pretend that they are decorating the kitchen!

As they become more confident, you could cut out some triangles and see if they can make them fit together.

What is tessellation?

When identical shapes fit together exactly without any gaps it is called tessellation. The word tessellation is thought to come from the Latin tessella which was the small, square stone or tile used in ancient mosaics. For young children the square is the best tessellating shape and lots of examples can be found such as floor and roof tiles, chess boards and pavements.

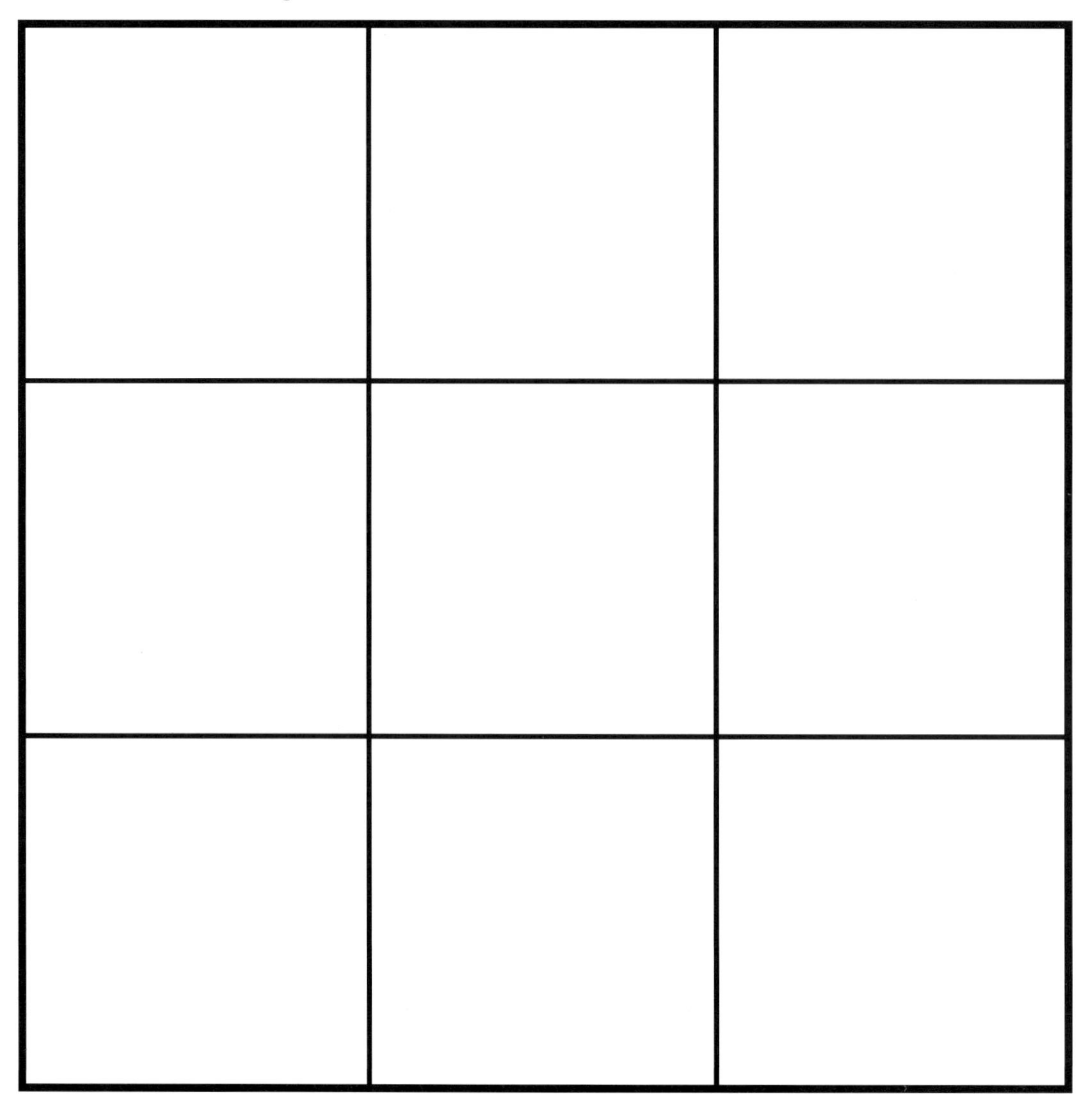

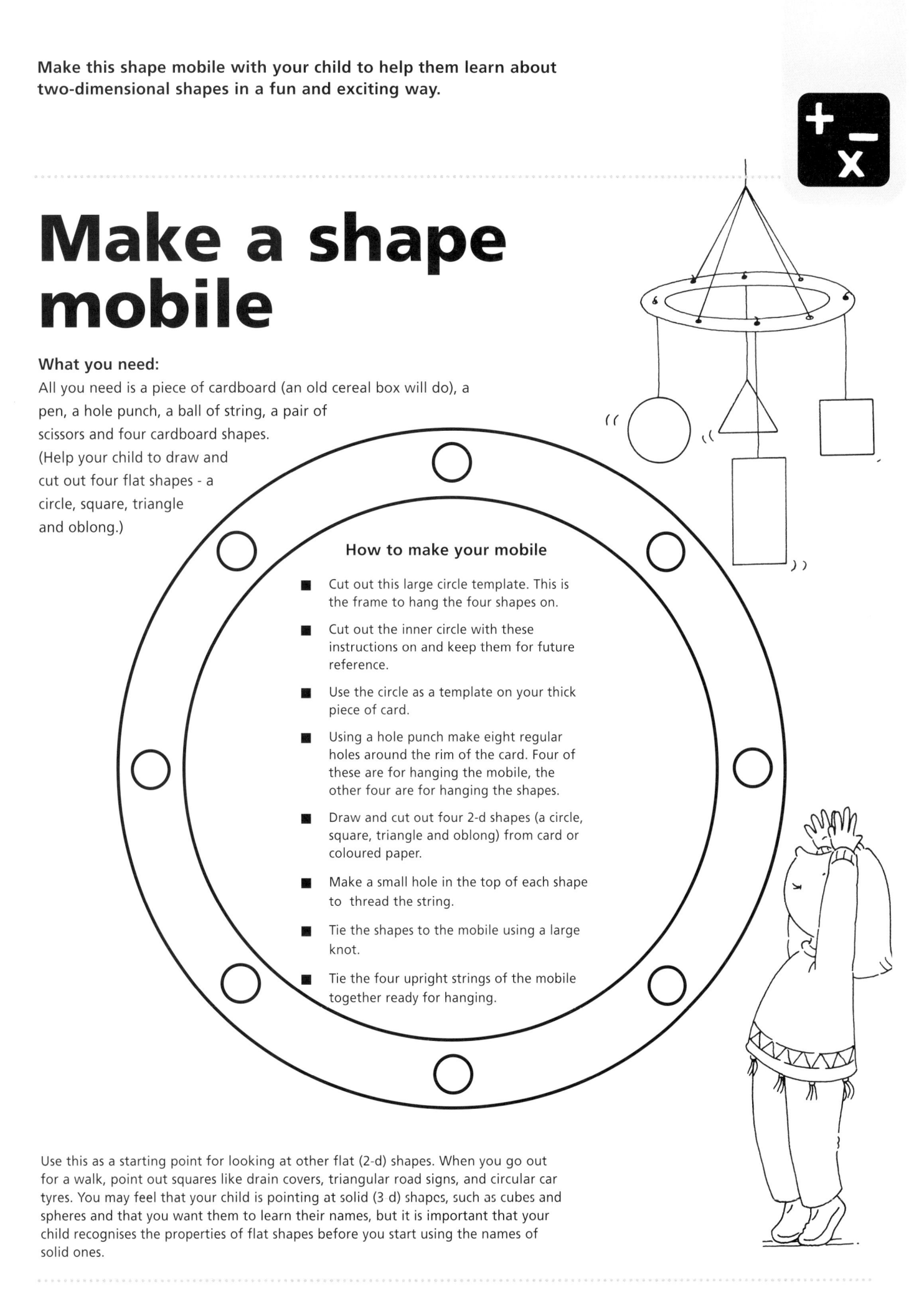

Make this shape mobile with your child to help them learn about two-dimensional shapes in a fun and exciting way.

Make a shape mobile

What you need:
All you need is a piece of cardboard (an old cereal box will do), a pen, a hole punch, a ball of string, a pair of scissors and four cardboard shapes. (Help your child to draw and cut out four flat shapes - a circle, square, triangle and oblong.)

How to make your mobile

- Cut out this large circle template. This is the frame to hang the four shapes on.
- Cut out the inner circle with these instructions on and keep them for future reference.
- Use the circle as a template on your thick piece of card.
- Using a hole punch make eight regular holes around the rim of the card. Four of these are for hanging the mobile, the other four are for hanging the shapes.
- Draw and cut out four 2-d shapes (a circle, square, triangle and oblong) from card or coloured paper.
- Make a small hole in the top of each shape to thread the string.
- Tie the shapes to the mobile using a large knot.
- Tie the four upright strings of the mobile together ready for hanging.

Use this as a starting point for looking at other flat (2-d) shapes. When you go out for a walk, point out squares like drain covers, triangular road signs, and circular car tyres. You may feel that your child is pointing at solid (3 d) shapes, such as cubes and spheres and that you want them to learn their names, but it is important that your child recognises the properties of flat shapes before you start using the names of solid ones.

Try using this template to make a simple pyramid, and help your child to recognise the shape and practise the names of colours

Make a pyramid

They can colour it in, then cut it out and glue it together.

You will perhaps need to make one first so that they can see what to do. It's quite fiddly - some young children may not have the fine motor skills to do the cutting, folding and gluing on their own and will need help.

Don't worry - they will still be learning important words to do with shape as you ask them to 'Colour in the red square' or 'Fold over the green triangle'.

At this stage children are just finding out about what different shapes look like.

For a more sturdy shape, use the outline as a template, drawing round it on to a piece of card.

Spot the shape

Go on a shape hunt with your child at home.

- Encourage them to spot cubes (stock cubes); cylinders (inside of a lavatory roll); spheres (balls); cuboids (boxes); a triangular prism (a Toblerone box); and a cone (party hat).
- Build on their knowledge of solid (3-d) shapes by drawing their attention to them whenever you are out and about. For example, a tent is a triangular prism, a block of flats is a cuboid and an oil drum is a cylinder.

green

blue   red   orange

yellow

Help your child to learn

Knowledge and Understanding of the World

In this area of learning children are developing the knowledge, skills and understanding that help them to make sense of the world:.

Exploring and investigating
They are finding out about all kinds of natural and made materials such as sand and water, playdough and clay. They notice things that are the same and different from each other, for example a car the same as yours, and start to ask questions about why things happen and how things work.

Designing and making
Young children enjoy playing with construction toys and will later be able to say what they have built or made. It is important for them to have the chance to use tools such as scissors and cutters.

Using technology
Your child will be interested in playing with remote control cars or working a tape recorder. Towards the end of the Reception year, they will be controlling a mouse on a computer or able to use a programmable toy.

Time and place
Children will be getting to know the area where they live, recognising local features and developing a sense of their community. They will talk about their environment and notice living things. Walks and trips to the park or shops will encourage this. They will also begin to distinguish past from present. Although at first they can be confused about 'today' and 'yesterday' they will eventually be able to talk about what they did at the weekend or on holiday.

Culture and beliefs
Your child will come to know that they are an individual with their own characteristics. They will start to understand that people celebrate a variety of festivals and develop respect for cultures and beliefs that are different to their own.

Too many children experience their local environment through a car window and get too little exercise. Explore your neighbourhood together and you'll be amazed at the sights and sounds!

Stop, look, listen

Children learn through doing - using all their senses. To understand the area where they live they need to walk around it with you so they can experience and talk about it. By helping your child to focus on and compare different features, you will be laying the foundations for science and geography as well as promoting a healthy life-style.

Can you walk to and from playgroup or pre-school? If it is too far to walk the whole way, stop the car a little distance away and walk the rest. As you are walking, encourage your child to focus on the world around them by asking a question like:

- How are people travelling? (Don't forget to look up at the sky.)

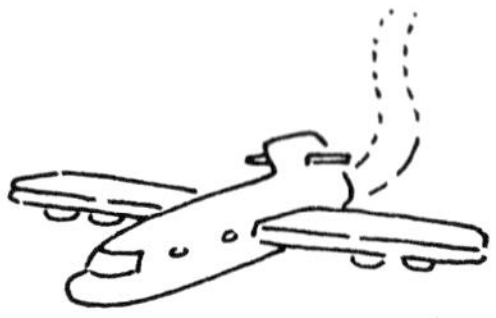

- What buildings can you see? What do you think goes on inside them? (Can you make time to go into public buildings you pass - such as a church, library, shop or post office? This will help your child learn more.)

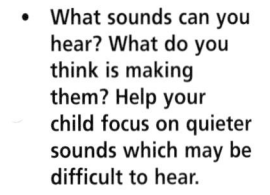

- What sounds can you hear? What do you think is making them? Help your child focus on quieter sounds which may be difficult to hear.

- Can you see people working outside? What are they doing?

- Can you smell anything? What do you think is making the smell?

At home, draw a rough map of your route and encourage your child to remember, and draw onto it, some of the things you saw or heard.

Help them compare other places you visit with where you come from - for example, 'How is the seaside/city different from where we live?' 'Are the shops the same or different?'

When crossing the road with children, try to get in the habit of saying the Green Cross Code together as a reminder

The Green Cross Code

Stand at a safe distance from the kerb.

Hold your grown-up's hand.

First find a safe place to cross, then stop.

Stop just before you get to the kerb.

Look all around for traffic and listen.

If traffic is coming, let it pass.

When it is safe, walk straight across the road. Do not run.

We often tell children 'Don't touch!' if something may be hot or easily broken. Yet we want children to explore their senses and realise that touching and feeling can pass on information as well as sight and hearing

Feely games

- Sort the washing or ironing into smooth clothes and rough clothes, silky or slippery things. Match socks into pairs by feel.

- Encourage your child to touch and feel. Can they identify parts of the face with their eyes shut? Can they tell the difference between a brother or sister, dad and mum?

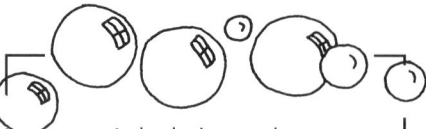

- At bath time: a dry sponge feels rough but soft and smooth when wet; shampoo or bubble bath feels slippery; bath toys are often hard and bumpy; and there's nothing nicer than fluffy towels or warm pyjamas.

- Play guessing games with the contents of the vegetable rack or fruit bowl. Use a scarf as a blindfold and feel the difference between an onion and an orange.

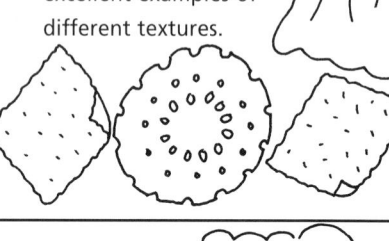

- Use household items to explore rubbing patterns - paper doilies, scraps of net curtain, colanders and wallpaper books are all excellent examples of different textures.

- Try a treasure hunt in the garden or park. Who can find five rough or bumpy items? (fir cones, stones, twigs) Or sort toys into groups by feel? (soft furry toys or hard and bumpy ones). You can do this with any collection of household items.

- Start collecting a bit box (bottle tops, buttons, packaging material, scraps of material). Not only can it be more fun than a toy box but it can be the best learning pack ever. Children can sort by texture, size, colour, material - the potential is endless.

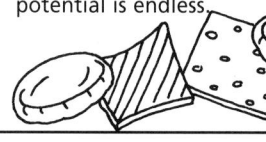

Science is all about finding out about the world and our place in it. It's about using our senses to explore new situations and experiences, discovering how things work or relate to each other, asking questions and developing ideas - children do it every day!

What do we mean by science?

Young children are great scientists - only we usually call it 'getting into everything'! What you need to do is help them develop their curiosity and skills so that they can begin to think and work in a logical way, begin to understand how the world works and how materials behave without destroying the wonder that is so precious to childhood.

In the kitchen
Many of the activities that go on every day in the home provide a wealth of science experiences. When you're cooking, let them see how the cake mixture changes after it has been in a hot oven. What happens when you put sugar into hot tea? It disappears or dissolves. Hold an ice cube and watch it melt (turn from a solid into liquid).

In the bathroom
When they're in the bath, give them lots of things to play with so they can find out which float and which sink. Blow bubbles. Watch the water going down the plug hole.

In the garden
When they're playing in the sand pit, children are investigating the properties of materials. How is dry sand different from wet sand? What can you do with one that you can't do with the other? What happens to the trolley or dolls' pram when they push it? Is it easier to push when it is full or empty? What happens to the ball if you kick it harder?

It is important to encourage children to have their own ideas and not be afraid to say them. Many children think that everything is either right or wrong. You need to help them realise that there may be different answers to some questions, particularly when carrying out an investigation. After all, if predictions are right every time, why bother to investigate?

> ### Learning from life
> The baby throwing a rattle from its pram is developing ideas about gravity. The child with ice-cream running down its chin is experiencing materials changing state. Seeing and smelling fruit and flowers, stroking a kitten or helping to care for a pet rabbit, help a child begin to appreciate the variety of life.

So that's gravity!

Questions, questions . . .
The sort of questions you ask are important.

What will happen if . . . ?

What do you think?

Why do you think that?

What is your idea?

These are key questions to get children thinking. Only give answers when you can see they are struggling. Experience will tell you when a child has gone as far as they can. Give them lots of praise and encouragement by saying things like 'That's a good idea'.

There are times when you need to give an answer, perhaps to old favourites such as 'Where does the sun go at night?'. Keep explanations clear and simple and don't be afraid to say 'I don't know, let's find out'. Use the opportunity to find the answer in a book, a CD-ROM or visit the local library. It is important for children to know that information can be found in other places and that they can find it for themselves.

The aim, always, is to encourage children to think for themselves, to question and to want to find out.

> ### All about ME!
> Talk about things your child is interested in. Don't forget, for very young children the world revolves around *me*, so that is a fairly good starting point! What are the various bits of *me* called? How do I move? Why do I need to eat and drink? How do I change? Is everybody the same? All this is science!

Help your child to learn

Here are some simple science investigations about freezing and melting. Most of them are everyday activities that you could try at home - believe it or not you'll be making a fun early start to chemistry!

What melts?

Science for breakfast

Make some toast. What can you spread on it when it is nice and hot? Try margarine, butter, honey and jam. What about Marmite, chocolate spread or peanut butter?

Get your child to look at all the things you are going to spread. Perhaps they could taste a tiny bit of each one on a spoon. Let them feel them in their mouth and on their tongue.

Which one do they think will melt the best on their toast? Is it going to be a thick one like peanut butter or chocolate spread, or a thin one like honey?

Get them to tell you what they think before they try.

The science

Freezing and melting are physical changes to materials which can be reversed. The materials can be made to change from a solid to a liquid and vice versa, over and over again. The change happens with the application of heat or cold. Ice melts when the environment which it is in is warmer than freezing, for example taking it out of the freezer into room temperature, putting it into a drink, or in the case of ice lollies, sucking it in a hot little mouth! Put back in the freezer, water or ice will re-freeze and this can be done as often as you like. (But beware! Don't eat anything which has been thawed and re-frozen.) Chocolate melts with the application of heat but then it can be left to solidify again.

Ice is nice!

A good way of helping children to understand that ice is frozen water and that when it melts it becomes water again is to make some ice lollies or cubes from diluted fruit squash. You can use the sticks from lollies you've bought if they're washed carefully. Use words like 'water', 'cold', 'warm', 'mix', 'freeze' and 'melt'.

Chocolate krispie cakes

Unlike ice, chocolate will not usually melt at room temperature - it needs the application of heat. A good way for children to find this out is to put a square of chocolate into each of two bowls, preferably transparent. Leave one bowl standing and place the other into another bowl of hot water (not dangerously hot!). Get the children to watch closely to see what is happening. Compare the square of chocolate in the bowl of hot water with the one left aside. Use words such as 'melt', 'heat', 'solid' and 'liquid'. If you don't want to waste the chocolate used for your science investigation, melt some more and make rice krispie or cornflake cakes. Stir enough rice krispies or cornflakes into the chocolate to coat them. Add a few sultanas to the mixture for an interesting variation. Divide the mixture into cake cases. Allow to set. Put some cakes into the refrigerator to set. Do those in the cold set more quickly than those left out?

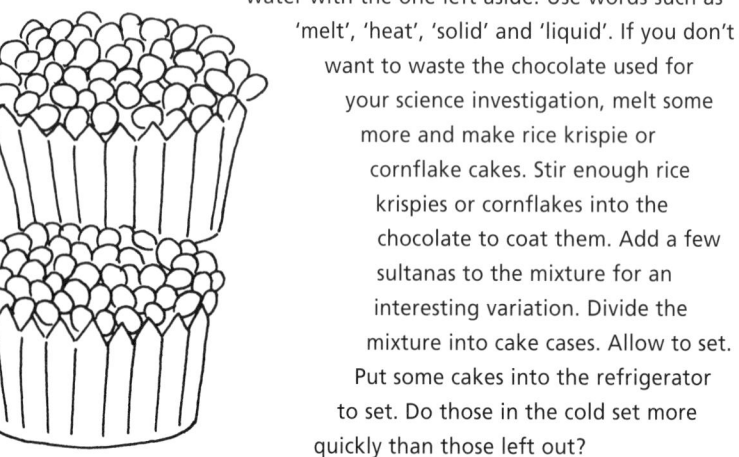

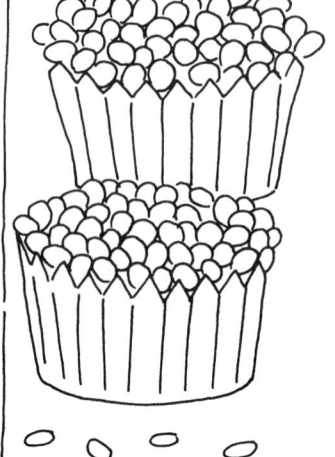

Help your child to learn

You don't need to be an expert on science to help your child learn more about the world around them, you just need to draw attention to what is happening. Next time you're out at the park or doing some cooking together, here are some ideas to think about

The world around us: forces

Forces play a huge part in our lives. We can't see them but we can certainly see their effects and we would definitely know if they weren't there!

What do children need to know?
An understanding of forces demands abstract thinking and young children are not ready for this, but they can experience and begin to describe what is happening when forces are acting. They can begin to think about cause and effect, for example 'If I want that trolley to move, I've got to push it'; 'If I drop my ball, it will fall to the floor'.

Children will do these things without necessarily thinking about them. You just need to draw their attention to what is happening and help them develop the language to describe it. They do not need to name different forces but they do need words such as 'pull', 'push', 'twist', 'fast', 'slow' and 'stop'.

Background information
Forces can:
- **start something moving**
  a push, a pull or gravity
- **make a moving thing go faster**
  increasing the push or pull
- **make a moving thing change direction**
  hit a ball with a bat
- **make a moving thing slow down**
  put the brakes on
- **make a moving thing stop**
  catch the ball
- **temporarily change the shape of an object**
  roll out the dough
- **permanently change the shape of an object**
  crush the garlic!

At the park
Forces are involved whenever anything is moving. Think of them as pushes, pulls or twists (a combination of push and pull). What is needed to make the swing swing or the see-saw move?

Blowing in the wind
Feel the push of the wind against your face. Run with a streamer and watch it move in the wind. Which way is the washing blowing? What does that tell you? What is the wind doing to the leaves on the trees? Watch the clouds - which way are they going?

Cooking
Think of the force you use to knead bread or mix pastry dough. How do you make the pastry flat? How do you change the lump of margarine into a fluffy cream? What do you do to crack an egg?

Help your child by making the most of common everyday occurrences and giving them the chance to look at, feel, smell and taste a whole variety of different materials

Finding out about materials

Every time you say to your child when you go out, 'Put your coat on, it's cold' or 'We don't need a coat or a cardigan today, it's lovely and warm' or 'We need the umbrella, it's raining', you are doing science! Your child will be learning about the materials that their coat, cardigan or umbrella are made of, that the coat and cardigan are made of materials which keep them warm and that the umbrella is waterproof.

Help them to learn by drawing their attention to this, by using the words 'warm' and 'waterproof' and asking them if they know what waterproof means. Ask them why we wear a coat when it is cold and a cardigan when it is not so cold. Can they tell you any other things which are waterproof? Can they tell you about other things which keep them warm like hats, gloves and scarves?

When you cook with your child, look closely at the ingredients you are going to use. Encourage them to feel, taste a tiny bit and smell. (Beware: don't allow children to taste uncooked egg.) What happens when you mix the things together? How is the raw cake mixture different from the cooked mixture? Has the mixture changed for ever or could we get the raw ingredients back?

In this way, you are letting your child focus on and experience how materials change when they are cooked. This is one of the early stages of chemistry! Cooking food brings about a chemical change in the ingredients which cannot be reversed.

Teach children not to taste or smell strange things unless an adult has told them that it is safe to do so.

Knowledge and Understanding of the World

At school or nursery, this kind of work relates to one of the Early Learning Goals for Knowledge and Understanding of the World which requires children to 'investigate objects and materials by using all of their senses as appropriate'. Children should also have opportunities to 'find out about, and identify some features of, living things, objects and events they observe'.

From a very early age, children are attracted to shiny objects which reflect the light and to mirrors in which they can see their own image. Help your child to learn about reflections by investigating shiny things around the home

Finding out about reflections

You can help your child become more observant by playing alongside them, making comments and asking questions. Help them to see how shiny objects reflect light and that sometimes our images are distorted if the shiny objects or mirrors are curved.

Blow bubbles and look at the reflections. What can they see? Do things look smaller or bigger than they really are?

Fill a dark coloured bowl or dish with water. Invite your child to look into it. What can they see? What happens when you make ripples on the water? Can they still see themselves?

Go on a mirror safari around the house. Try to find the following:

■ shaving mirror

■ make-up mirror

■ car mirror

■ wing mirror

■ hall mirror

What can your child notice about their face when they look in the shaving mirror or the wing mirror?

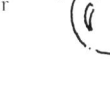

Encourage them to look at themselves in other shiny objects. Try:

■ a soup spoon/front and back;

■ the shiny kettle;

■ the TV screen when it is switched off;

■ shiny paper;

■ Christmas baubles, and so on.

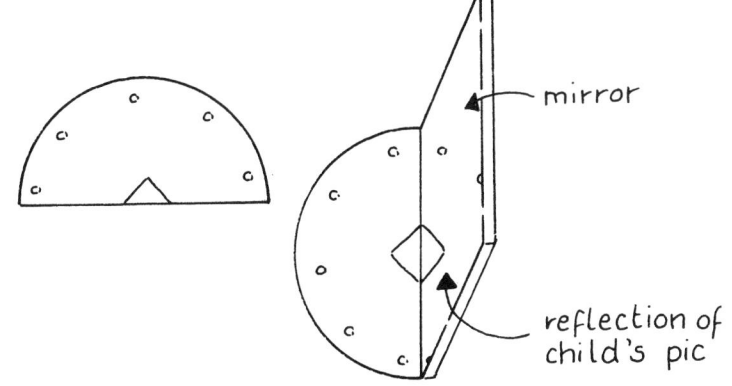

Making halves into wholes

Draw a semi-circle on a plain sheet of paper. Ask your child to draw a pattern in the semi-circle. Show them how to use a mirror to make the half circle into a whole. You can also do this by drawing half of a face, an animal or a person.

Now try making your own half pictures.

In many homes children play with magnetic letters and numbers. They will have seen magnets on fridges and memo boards and may have construction kits with magnetic components. You can help them to learn more about magnets by carrying out some of the following activities

The magic of magnets

Try out some of your fridge magnets on objects around the kitchen, for example pots, pans, utensils, baking trays and so on.

Try them on cupboard doors, plastic boxes and wooden spoons.

Talk to your child about the materials the objects are made from.

Play a choosing game and ask your child to find objects made of different materials - metal, plastic, wood, paper. Talk to them about the materials and name them.

Put a variety of materials on a tray and ask your child to guess whether or not they will be attracted to the magnet. Test to see if they were right. (You might like to pick objects such as hair grips, paper clips, drawing pins, wooden beads and scraps of paper.)

Note: The magnets children use at school are made of metal but fridge magnets are often made of ceramic or plastic material which contains magnetic substances.

Remember
Keep magnets away from bank and credit cards as well as cassette tapes and watches.

What are magnets?
Don't feel that you have to teach your child these ideas. It is enough at this stage for them to experiment, investigate and talk about what they see. They will have lots of opportunities when they are older to build on these early ideas.

- Magnets attract iron and steel (in other words, not all metals)
- Magnetic forces can make things move/lift things up
- Magnets have two poles - one north-seeking, the other south-seeking
- A magnet can make objects made of iron and steel into temporary magnets
- The stored magnetic energy in a magnet is due to the special arrangement of the atoms inside the iron or steel used to make the magnet. That is why if magnets are dropped or knocked they lose the magnetic effect because the atoms are disarranged.

Help your child to learn

Water play really begins at home - in the bath, in the kitchen sink and in the paddling pool during the summer. To make the most of this fun activity you do not need to spend a fortune. Here are some ideas

Messing about with water

Washing up
Most small children love to be by your side at the sink to 'help' with the washing-up and will, given the chance, become able at handling wet cutlery and crockery. If you are worried about breakages, provide them with an extra bowl on a small table and a set of plastic crockery so that they can share the experience with you. It all helps to develop essential manipulative skills.

Your child learns all sorts of things from playing with water:

- to control their movements, exercising smaller muscles
- that volume can change
- that shape can be relative and fluid
- that weight and balance are related
- what 'more' looks like
- what 'less' means in practice
- that some objects float and others sink
- that some objects sometimes float and sometimes sink
- that big into small does not go
- that small into big often goes

Equipment for free!
Why not collect washing-up liquid bottles, empty squash bottles, yoghurt pots and other containers? Punch holes in some of them, keep the lids for others, keep different sized ones and offer plastic cups and jugs at the same time.

Make a water garden
Children love to make a water garden. Help them gather the necessary items and then let them experiment. This can often take several hours as items are arranged and re-arranged until they are happy with their creation. Let them experiment - this is all part of the fun. Plastic tanks are readily available at most pet shops (they are often used for pet mice and are reasonably priced). They can be filled with live fish and plants or with plastic fish (a piece of cotton tied around the fish which is then attached to a stone will keep it floating in the water rather than on the top), plants collected from the river and stones from the garden. Once arranged, the tank can be filled with water (from the river or pond if you have one nearby) and the children can then study its progress. Don't forget to return any wildlife to its original home!

You can turn even the most ordinary household chore into a scientific experiment simply by asking questions and encouraging your child to take notice and think about what is happening. Who would have thought that washing up could be so educational? All of these ideas are to do with floating and sinking

Floating and sinking

- Talk about things that float on water.

- Guess if an object will float or not.

- Try it and see what happens.

- Help your child to understand words like:
  float, sink, heavy, light, surface, above, below, deep, shallow.

What will they learn?
Children will see that small, heavy objects tend to sink and that larger, light objects tend to float.

They need to know that whether an object floats is not related to size - a large, heavy object such as a ship can float. Nor is it related to shape. Test a number of round objects - a marble, a ball bearing, a golf ball, a plastic ball, an orange, an onion.

In this way children will begin to develop some of the concepts that they will need later on.

In the washing-up bowl
Make a collection of objects - paper, a stone, polystyrene, wood, fabric, a metal object. Let the children guess which will float, then try out each object in turn.

At the seaside
Talk about boats, yachts, seaweed - or use a picture book. Do they realise that an iceberg floats? Try floating an ice cube in water.

At the swimming pool
Look at what people use to support themselves, like arm bands, rubber rings and polystyrene floats. Why is it harder to walk in water than on land? Push a piece of polystyrene or another large object that floats under the water - what do they feel?

In the bath
Compare what happens to a plastic boat, a sponge and a piece of soap. Float a dry sponge on the surface. Push it under the water and squeeze it. Watch the air bubbles come out. Try floating it again. Float a plastic bottle, then fill it with water in stages. Each time, replace the cap and watch what happens when you put it in the water.

In the park
Notice what is floating on puddles or in a pond, such as leaves, frogspawn, some ducks, bubbles or a crisp bag.

Have you noticed how many empty packets and boxes you throw away each week? Have you ever thought of recycling them into rockets or lorries or skyscrapers? They make the perfect material for your child to use for a simple activity which will help them think about design as well as practise valuable skills such as cutting and joining - the first steps in technology

Making things from junk

Start collecting your empty packets over the next few days and weeks, for example, cereal boxes, tea packets, toothpaste boxes, stock cube boxes, yoghurt pots, round cheese boxes. Collect as many different shapes and sizes as possible. You will also need some washable glue, brushes or spreaders, masking tape, and powder paints if you want to paint the finished models.

Junk will begin to take on a whole new meaning. The problems start when you find yourself buying things you don't usually buy just because of the box!

- Cover a table with a plastic cloth or newspaper. Lay out all the boxes and ask your child what they would like to make. At first they may just enjoy sticking the boxes together. For young children, the process is often more important than the product! Be careful not to expect too much from them before they are ready.

- After some time of 'just sticking' they may decide to make a model of something - perhaps a bus, a house, a rocket and so on. Try to help, without taking over, so the finished model really is their own work. You could say something like 'How about these round boxes for the wheels?' or show them some new fixing skills as and when they are appropriate, such as using masking tape or elastic bands to hold boxes together while the glue dries, or how to make holes in card by pushing a pencil through onto a lump pf playdough.

- Let them paint their finished models if they want to.

Helpful tip: The paint will stick to shiny surfaces and plastic better if you mix it with some glue.

Who needs expensive toys and equipment when you can make good use of discarded household items? It's amazing what you can do with a few lids and tops!

Taking the lid off things!

Make a collection of as many different types of lids and tops as you can find for your child to explore and play with. They are a really cheap but useful resource. They can be off anything and any shape or size. Here are some ideas:

- bottle tops
- tops off washing/cleaning products (some have little measuring cups)
- butter/margarine lids
- coffee/sauce/spread/jam-jar lids
- lids off deodorants/hair products/toothpaste tubes
- lids and tops that flip up, screw on, press on, pop on/off
- lids made from all kinds of materials - metal, plastic, silver, ceramic, cork (old teapot and saucepan lids). What about a glass stopper? Children need to learn that some materials need to be handled with care.

Wash them and make sure that they are clean before you give them to your child.

Here are some activities you can use them for

Empty the lids out on a table or the floor and let your child play with them. Can they work out what they all are? Sit with them and talk. What could this one be for? How can you tell? How does it work? Have you seen it on anything at home? What is it made of? What shape is it? What would happen if we had no lids? You can have hours of fun just exploring the different items and guessing what they're from!

Sort out a collection of the same lids (coffee type lids are ideal). Stick some coloured spots, numbers or small pictures on the inside of the lids. Be sure to make up doubles (or other sets). When you're ready to play - spread the lids over the table/floor face down and let your child try to find the matching pairs or sets.

Put a few lids into a shoe bag or pillow case so that your child can't see them. Show them one that is the same and ask them to feel for an identical one from the bag - no peeping!

Note: check the lids regularly to make sure they are clean and have no broken, sharp edges. Be careful not to give very young children small lids that they could swallow.

As children explore their environment, they meet things that puzzle them and often want to know why something looks or behaves like it does. The way in which you respond to their questions will not only provide answers (if you know them!) but can also develop a positive attitude to learning

Learning to solve problems

Young children learn in many ways - through playing with different materials, by watching others and talking about things they do and see. One way that is important is through solving problems, since this develops children's thinking skills.

At school or in the nursery, adults encourage children to try to do things for themselves. If a problem arises, children will be helped to solve it. You know your child really well. You recognise when your child needs time to think something out for themselves and when they need help.

Problems happen every day. Your child may be able to tackle some on their own but will need help to solve others. There are many situations when you can help your child become a confident problem-solver.

When three-year-old Joanne is putting on her socks, she often gets the heel at the front of the foot. It is easier and much quicker to twist the sock around for her but Joanne's parents want her to be as independent as possible, so they give her the time to find the part of her foot that matches the bulge in the sock. By doing this, Joanne is learning to use clues that help her solve her problem as well as finding out about a part of her body.

Memory plays an important part in solving a problem successfully and there are a number of games that children enjoy and which will develop a child's ability to remember. Kim's game involves looking carefully at a few objects on a tray, covering them up and trying to remember them. Another favourite, which could be kept quite short, is 'I went shopping and bought a...', each player takes it in turns to repeat the list and add an item. Card games such as 'find the pairs' can also be kept simple and yet encourage the use of memory.

Everyday experiences can be turned into problem-solving exercises which develop learning. Encourage your child to help with putting away the groceries. How items fit onto a shelf develops an understanding of space. If a drink is spilled, children can decide the best way to mop it up - cloth or paper towel. Which is more absorbent?

Bath time provides opportunities for setting challenges - Can your child find a way to sink the boat? The water's too hot, what should we do?

Four-year-old Matthew has made a cake with his grandma who encourages him to use his understanding of number to decide how many pieces they need to share it with the family.

How many times have you asked your child what they have done at pre-school or school and been met with the reply 'We just played!'? Don't let this worry you - it's a good sign

Playing and learning

You almost certainly had a lot of freedom to play as a child, but you may worry about your own child playing – particularly if they are playing in nursery or school. Don't they do any work? Shouldn't they be learning to read and write? But remember that children growing up today have much less freedom than we did to play within their local community.

Why play?
Play helps young children develop relationships with others, express their feelings, make sense of their (often confusing) world, become imaginative and creative, use language for different purposes and develop thinking skills.

When the staff who work with your child talk about learning through play, trust what they say. They are sharing with you what is quite clear in research – that young children who experience high quality play do better, both academically and socially, in later life than those who have been taught formally. This is because children who are encouraged to learn through well-planned play are more motivated and less likely to become bored.

Encouraging your child's play
Children's play is inspired by their experiences and the people they have to play with. When you take your child on outings to shops, the seaside, on a train journey or to a café or restaurant, they will want to relive these experiences in play. After a visit to a café, you could encourage your child to make a menu so you can play cafés together. Make time to play with your child. Let your child take the lead and you will be amazed by what they know and can do.

Ask staff in your child's nursery or school to tell you about what they have been learning through play. Talk to your child about this, and try to give them some similar opportunities at home. Remember that, although learning through play may be hard to see, it is likely to be long-lasting and much more worthwhile than colouring in a worksheet.

What kinds of play do young children need?
Children need to learn through play, indoors and outdoors, alone and with friends. Make sure your child has the following play opportunities both at home and in their nursery or school:

- Exploring and creating with natural materials such as sand, water, clay, mud, wood, leaves, shells and pebbles.

- Building and making things with boxes, blankets, bricks and construction kits - often to create imaginary worlds such as dens or space ships.

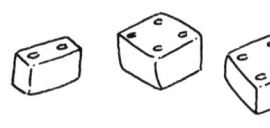

- Physical play on tricycles, trucks or climbing equipment.

- Taking on roles within the adult world (such as pretending to be mum and dad, the doctor, vet, or shopkeeper) or from the world of stories (such as the three bears). This kind of play is essential if children are to become successful story-tellers and writers.

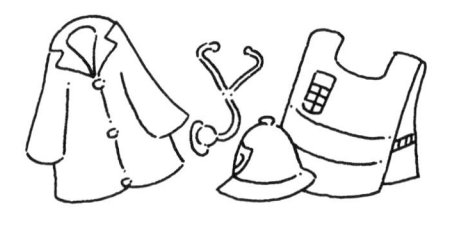

- Exploring small-scale environments such as the dolls' house, railway set or farm set.

Play materials do not have to be expensive. Remember how many uses you found for the old tin tray, cardboard box or broom!

Learning colours is one of the first skills a toddler can achieve. You can help you child with this - but remember it should be fun!

Learning about colour

The most important thing is spending time with your child, doing things together and playing together.

Second most important is talking about the things that you do together and about the world around you. Listen carefully to what they have to say and what they are interested in.

There are so many things to learn, 'Is this a dog or a cat?' or 'Is that a chair or a sofa?' and 'Is this a dress or a skirt?' At this stage, colour is just another thing to say, usually just after someone else has said it or because they like the sound of the word. However, if you continue to include colours in your descriptions of things, your child will gradually begin to make the connections they need to know that this is red and that is green.

When children start to get the idea about what colours are, you can begin to expect them to be more active. Offer them some coloured crayons and ask 'Which colour do you want?' At first they will just point and you can name their choice.

Later they will begin to guess colour names for themselves and you need to be positive, encouraging and reinforcing the correct names without seeming critical.

Children learn:
- **Through play**
- **Through repetition**
- **Through language that supports their play**
- **With the support of caring adults**

Ways you can help
- By giving objects their colours as you talk about them, for example: 'Joe's door is black', 'That car is red', 'Put your red boots on', or 'Would you like a lovely orange carrot?'.

- By pointing out colours around you, for example: 'Look at the red bus', 'The yellow digger', 'The green grass and blue sky'.

- By pointing out things that are the same colour, for example: 'Your coat is blue like mummy's' or 'Oh look, you've used green in your painting just like our kettle' and repeat the colours for emphasis as you point to them, 'blue blue', 'green green'.

Children take a long time to grasp the idea of colour but there are many ways to help them learn

Colour your conversation

Seeing red
- Visit somewhere which strongly connects to your chosen colour, green for the park, red for the fire station or post office.

Spot the colour
- You could have a colour day at home. Let your child pick something to wear in the chosen colour. Play 'Spot the colour' or 'Colour I spy' ('I spy something red', for example) on the way to nursery or the shops.
If you drive, point out the colour of traffic lights and what they mean or the red or green crossing symbols.
Have a colour hunt in the house and collect items - toys, buttons, kitchen utensils, clothes - all of the same colour.

Cooking in technicolour
- You could try some simple cooking and add food colouring to cake mix or icing and decorate the finished result with small coloured sweets. If you feel really brave add the colouring to mashed potatoes: it can sometimes be the bizarre which sticks in a child's mind!

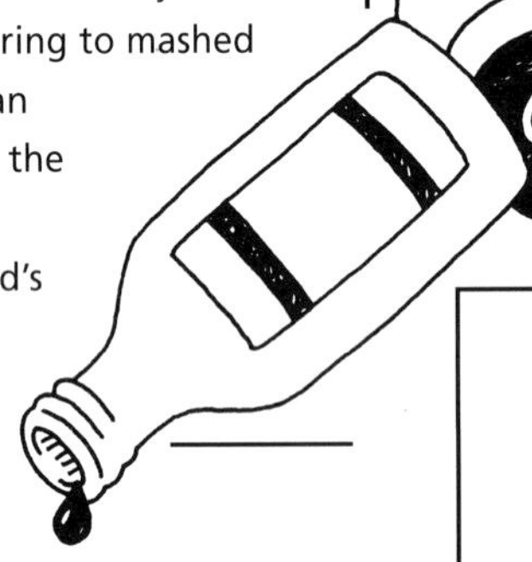

Special stories
- Visit your local library and choose a special story book connected to your chosen colour. What about 'Little Red Riding Hood'? or a book with a big red and black ladybird on the cover?

You don't need expensive equipment or toys to help your child, just a little time and thought to say the obvious. Add colour to your conversation - 'We're going on the green bus', 'Put on your red boots'.

When they are outdoors children can run around and let off steam but they can also exercise and develop their minds as well as their bodies

The great outdoors

Whether at pre-school, at home or in the park, outdoors can be a whole new world for young children, a place to explore and discover, to question and wonder, to imagine and dream. Believe it or not, moving about outside can have as much to do with maths and science as building strength and stamina, confidence and well-being.

Digging and mixing

Set aside a small area of garden where your child can dig. Let them have some small but real tools, some containers, flower pots, sieves, and a watering can and let their imagination run wild! It might be finding worms or small insects; sorting and washing stones and arranging them in patterns; or discovering hidden treasure. Let them add water and mix it with the soil to make pretend dinner or cement.

Freezing and melting

Leave some containers of water outside on a frosty night. Children will be amazed to find the solid blocks of ice, to see the bubbles, to find out that thin sheets of ice are transparent. Try dropping salt onto the ice and listen to the sound and watch what happens. Bring a lump indoors and time (measure) how long it takes to melt compared with the ice outdoors. (Transformation - how materials can change - is an important part of scientific learning.)

Painting and decorating

Buckets, water, large decorating brushes and a paint roller can provide endless opportunities for 'painting'. Walls, fences and paving stones can be covered over and marks and pictures can appear then disappear as the water dries up. This is ideal for large sweeping arm movements, and for talking about evaporation (Where has the water gone?)

Throwing and hitting

Hang some empty plastic bottles and containers on a washing line. See if your child can aim and throw soft balls to hit them. Alternatively encourage them to hit the containers with a ping pong bat (a version of swing ball). This can help develop physical skills, co-ordination, estimating distance and ideas about forces. It is ideal for children who love to throw and hit.

You don't need to have a garden to make good use of the outdoors. Giving a child a tub for growing things on a balcony, fixing a bird feeder to the window, finding insects in the park, talking about the moon and the stars at night are just a few ways in which the outdoors can be explored as a source of wonder.

Help your child to learn

You don't have to live in the countryside to go on a nature walk - you can still look out for mosses growing on walls, weeds growing through cracks in the pavements or birds such as pigeons and starlings. Explore some local wasteland for caterpillars or beetles or go to your local park

Getting back to nature!

Children are naturally curious. Information they collect on walks helps them to understand the world around them and their place in it. Young children learn by using their senses and by talking about what they find.

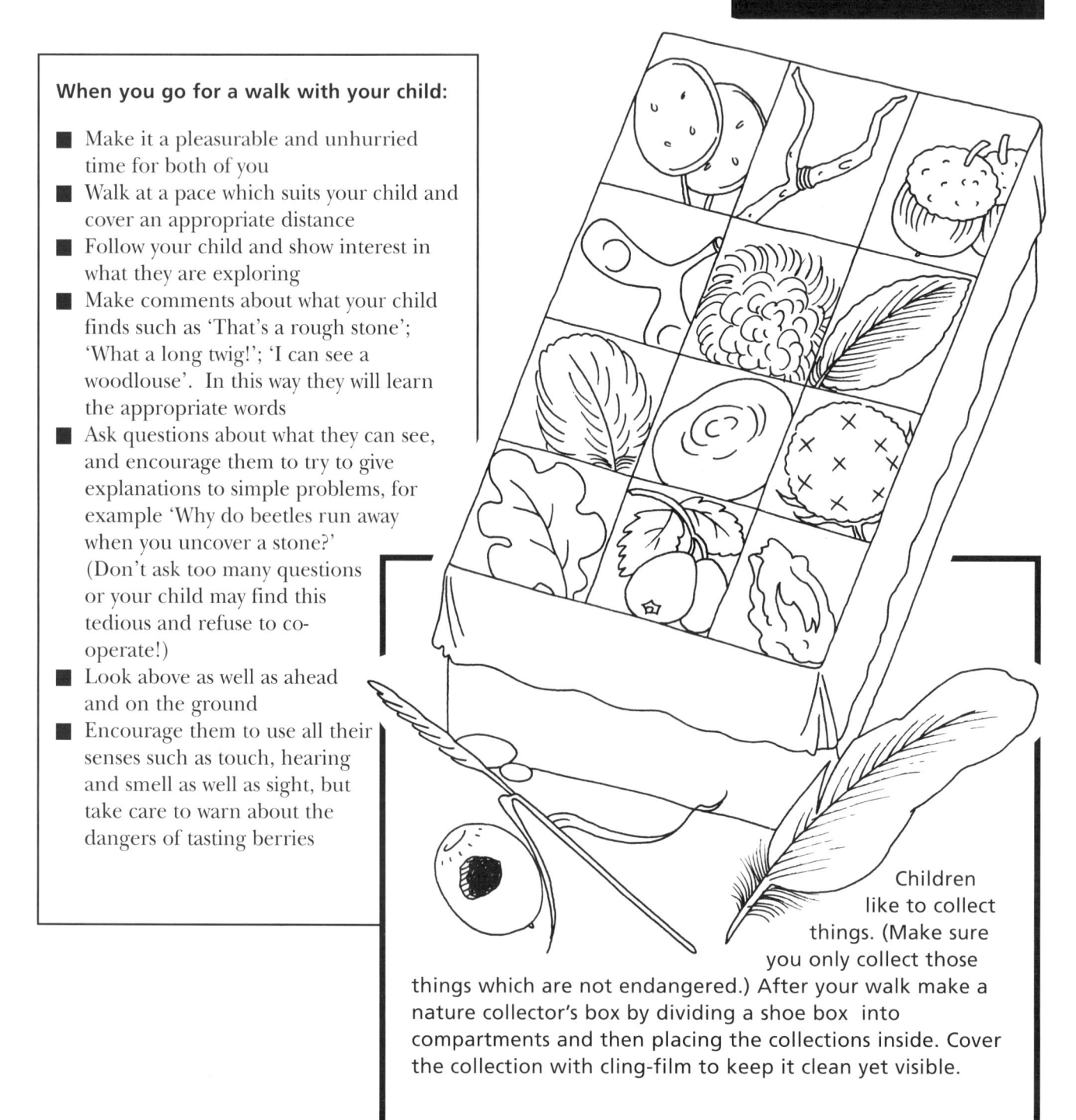

When you go for a walk with your child:

- Make it a pleasurable and unhurried time for both of you
- Walk at a pace which suits your child and cover an appropriate distance
- Follow your child and show interest in what they are exploring
- Make comments about what your child finds such as 'That's a rough stone'; 'What a long twig!'; 'I can see a woodlouse'. In this way they will learn the appropriate words
- Ask questions about what they can see, and encourage them to try to give explanations to simple problems, for example 'Why do beetles run away when you uncover a stone?' (Don't ask too many questions or your child may find this tedious and refuse to co-operate!)
- Look above as well as ahead and on the ground
- Encourage them to use all their senses such as touch, hearing and smell as well as sight, but take care to warn about the dangers of tasting berries

Children like to collect things. (Make sure you only collect those things which are not endangered.) After your walk make a nature collector's box by dividing a shoe box into compartments and then placing the collections inside. Cover the collection with cling-film to keep it clean yet visible.

Children are fascinated by things that grow and change and there are lots of things you can do with your child to develop their interest in gardening, even if you don't have a garden

How does your garden grow?

Getting started
A good way to spark off an interest in growing things is to buy a couple of gardening magazines with lots of bright, colourful pictures in. Look at them together, talk about what you see and cut out pictures to make collages or plant labels. There's no need to spend a lot of money – one of the best places to find gardening books and magazines is charity shops and jumble sales. Let your child help you look for them.

How gardening can help your child
- Gardening will help your child develop their language and communication skills, as they tell you what they want to do (or have done).

- It will give them the chance to be creative as they design a garden or make pots to grow things in.

- Caring for a living thing will get your child thinking about their own role in your family and maybe the wider world.

- Gardening is great for using some of the muscles your child will need as they become more adventurous and active.

- Success is important to small children – their confidence will be boosted by seeing a tiny seed that they planted grow into a giant sunflower, all through their own efforts.

Cut pictures of tools, flowers, pots and bags of compost from your magazines to make a gardening poster or picture. Write the names of the items on, too, to help your child get to know the alphabet and words to do with gardening.

Gardening in containers
If you don't have an outdoor space to garden in, what about gardening in containers? Pots can be kept outdoors or indoors. The main thing to remember is to have drainage holes in the base of the container. Other than that, let your child's imagination run wild! See how many different kinds of container you can find, decorating each one with gardening themes. You could use:

- Old Wellington boots
- Old sinks or toilets
- Troughs
- Tyres
- Chimney pots
- Hollowed out tree trunk
- Buckets

Growing plants from seed
Collect some different containers for growing seeds, such as margarine tubs, foil food trays or yoghurt pots. Help your child decorate them using paints, fabric and collage. Visit your nearest garden centre to choose seeds with your child. You'll also need some compost.

- Make holes in the bottom of the containers and place compost in a layer. Most seeds are sown close to the surface – check each packet for instructions.

- Sow different seeds in each container, covering them loosely with a clear plastic bag (such as a sandwich bag) to make a mini-greenhouse.

- Place the containers on saucers and put them on a sunny windowsill. Keep them moist by watering into the saucer to avoid damaging the new seedlings.

- When the seedlings have grown to about 8 or 10 cm, you can plant them out into your garden or into bigger containers.

87
Help your child to learn

Gardening is fun and it's educational. You don't need any expensive tools or equipment - or even a garden! Here are some straightforward mini-projects to try out at home with your child

Get into gardening

Cress egg-heads
- Grow cress on damp cotton wool in the bottom of empty eggshells.
- Draw funny faces on the shells. When the cress 'hair' has grown, you can cut it and eat it.
- Show your child the furry root hairs of the cress seeds growing on the cotton wool.
- If you leave the egg-heads on a light window sill the cress will grow towards the light.

Bushy tops
Show children how fruit and vegetables that you buy from the shops are still alive.
- Cut the top 2.5 cm off a pineapple, carrot or parsnip and place it onto the surface of some wet vermiculite (see 'What you will need').
- Keep it damp and soon the tops will start to sprout.

Pips and stones
Show your child where to find the seeds in different fruit, such as apples, pears, peaches, cherries, grapes, and so on. Then plant them. Children will enjoy seeing them grow.
- Plant lots because a few won't grow.
- Be patient because some take a long while to germinate.

Mini-veg for maximum fun
- Look out for seed varieties of miniature vegetables such as carrots, lettuce, cauliflower, peppers and cherry tomatoes.
- Grow them at home on the patio.
- Remember to identify the parts of the plants: carrots are special roots; lettuce are edible leaves; and the cauliflower head is a flower.
- Children are far more likely to eat the miniature veg if they have grown it themselves.

Don't bin it ... plant in it!
- See how many unusual planting containers you and the children can make from the things you would normally throw away.
- Make sure you wash any container thoroughly before you use it.
- Try the following: margarine tubs, ice-cream tubs, moulded plastic packaging from Easter eggs or toys; plastic egg cartons.

What you will need
- Cotton wool, egg shells, felt pens, cress seeds.
- Pineapple, carrot or parsnip, vermiculite (a granular growing material available from the garden centre).
- Selection of fruits (for example, apple, pear grape, peach, cherry), small pots, compost.
- Miniature vegetable seeds, patio pots, compost.

You may have looked inside a flower hundreds of times or marvelled at how a bird builds its nest, but for your child these are new and wonderful experiences! Here are some other scientific discoveries you can share

Finding out about plants and animals

Children are natural scientists, forever asking questions about the world around them. You play an important role in nurturing this curiosity by giving your child the chance to explore and investigate what might seem to us common everyday objects, events and experiences.

Living things are part of our world and we all need to learn about them and understand what they - and we! - need to survive.

Asking the right questions at the right time is the key to encouraging a child's thinking.

Plants and flowers
In the garden or on outings, look for different plants. Ask your child:

- How are they different?
- Do they all have flowers?
- Where are the flowers on trees?
- Are all their leaves the same shape or colour?
- How many different ones can you find in your garden?

Don't worry too much about identifying the particular species, though they may enjoy learning the names of some common plants such as daisy, buttercup and daffodil. The important thing is that they are able to tell the difference between, say, a flower and a leaf.

Encourage children not to pick wild flowers or tear leaves from trees. It is never too early to think about conservation!

Grow your own!
If possible, give your child a small corner of the garden, an old sink or big tub to grow things for themselves. Explain that seeds grow into new plants and that different seeds grow into different plants.

Lettuce and radish grow quite quickly. A cherry tomato is fun and you can get some varieties such as Tumbler that will even grow in a hanging basket. A wigwam of canes in a tub will support a crop of runner beans. Who knows, growing your own may even tempt the reluctant vegetable eater!

Grow a potato in a large tub or bucket. Fill the bucket about half full of compost and plant a potato in it. As the leaves begin to show through, cover it with more compost. Do this two or three times more and in a couple of months or so you will be able to tip the whole thing out onto a plastic sheet and find the buried treasure - lots of little potatoes. The longer you leave it, the bigger the potatoes will get.

When you're gardening together, ask your child to name the different parts of a plant - leaf, flower, stem. Where are the roots?

Safety note:
Children should know that we eat plants or parts of plants but that it is not safe to eat things we don't recognise.

Caring for animals
If you have a pet, encourage your child to become involved in its care. Grooming, feeding and exercising can be fun for all concerned and begin to instil a sense of responsibility.

Whenever you're out in the park or garden, look for minibeasts - ants, spiders, woodlice, butterflies, snails.

- How many legs can you see?
- Do they all have wings?
- What do you think they eat?
- Where do you think they live?
- What do you think their babies look like?
- How are they different to us?

Whether it's a budgie, a goldfish or a pedigree poodle, the family pet can be the source of valuable learning experiences for your child as well as a much-loved companion

All creatures great and small

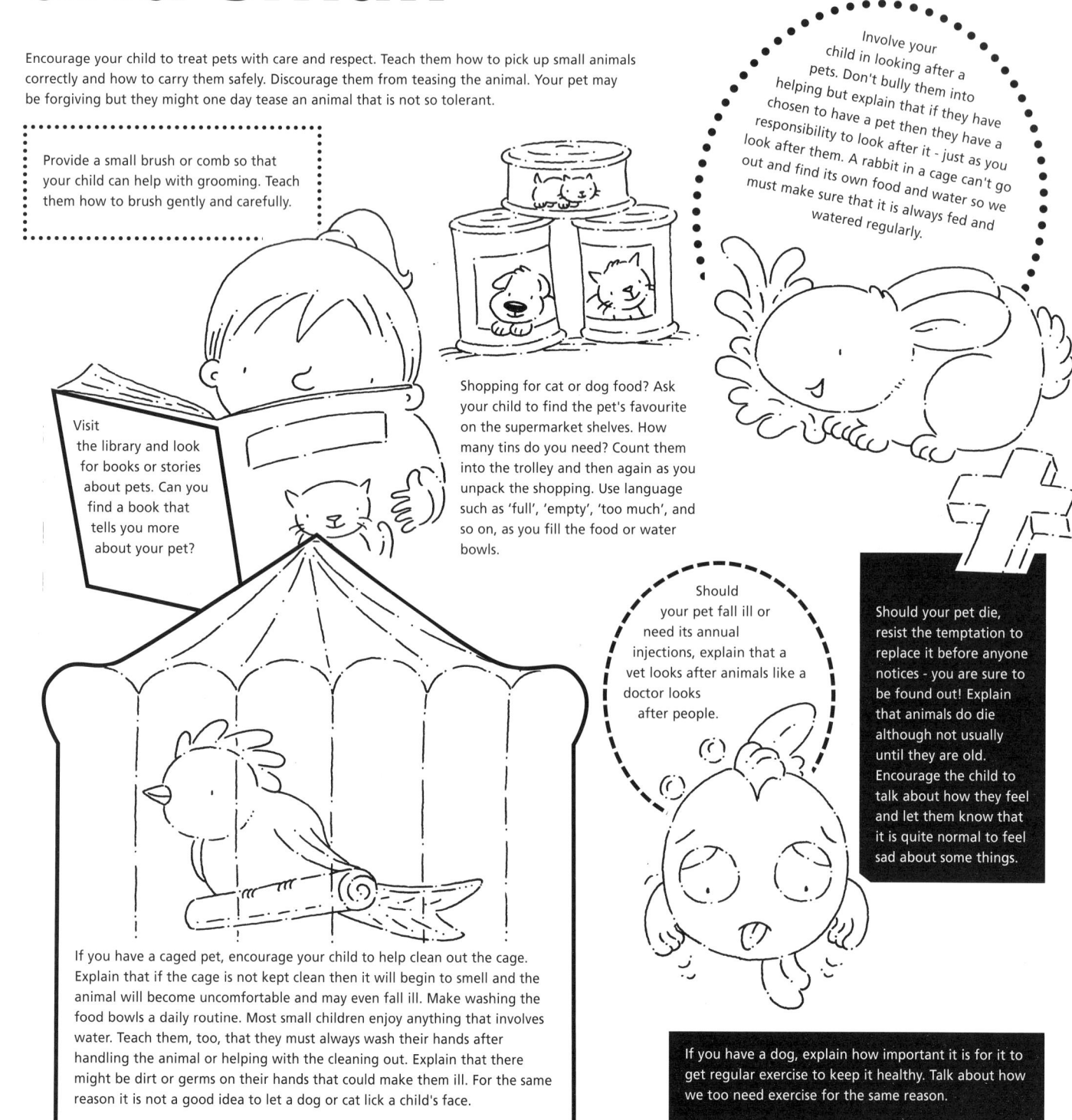

Encourage your child to treat pets with care and respect. Teach them how to pick up small animals correctly and how to carry them safely. Discourage them from teasing the animal. Your pet may be forgiving but they might one day tease an animal that is not so tolerant.

Provide a small brush or comb so that your child can help with grooming. Teach them how to brush gently and carefully.

Involve your child in looking after a pets. Don't bully them into helping but explain that if they have chosen to have a pet then they have a responsibility to look after it - just as you look after them. A rabbit in a cage can't go out and find its own food and water so we must make sure that it is always fed and watered regularly.

Visit the library and look for books or stories about pets. Can you find a book that tells you more about your pet?

Shopping for cat or dog food? Ask your child to find the pet's favourite on the supermarket shelves. How many tins do you need? Count them into the trolley and then again as you unpack the shopping. Use language such as 'full', 'empty', 'too much', and so on, as you fill the food or water bowls.

Should your pet fall ill or need its annual injections, explain that a vet looks after animals like a doctor looks after people.

Should your pet die, resist the temptation to replace it before anyone notices - you are sure to be found out! Explain that animals do die although not usually until they are old. Encourage the child to talk about how they feel and let them know that it is quite normal to feel sad about some things.

If you have a caged pet, encourage your child to help clean out the cage. Explain that if the cage is not kept clean then it will begin to smell and the animal will become uncomfortable and may even fall ill. Make washing the food bowls a daily routine. Most small children enjoy anything that involves water. Teach them, too, that they must always wash their hands after handling the animal or helping with the cleaning out. Explain that there might be dirt or germs on their hands that could make them ill. For the same reason it is not a good idea to let a dog or cat lick a child's face.

If you have a dog, explain how important it is for it to get regular exercise to keep it healthy. Talk about how we too need exercise for the same reason.

Empty plastic or waxed-card containers and cartons make great bird feeders. Why not make some at home, then hang them out with some seeds, peanuts, crumbs, scraps of fat or suet and see how many different birds you attract

Make a bird feeder

What you need
Waxed-card long-life milk or fruit juice cartons are perhaps the easiest to use. More permanent, large feeders can be made from plastic containers, such as 2-litre milk or detergent cartons, though you will need to do the cutting.

What to do
You will need to cut the first hole in one or more sides with a sharp knife. Your child can then make them bigger with round-ended scissors. The idea is to make openings in the sides so that it becomes a lantern-shaped mini bird table. You could let your child paint the feeders, but you'll need a waterproof paint - or decorate them with sticky-backed plastic. See if the colour makes a difference - do the birds prefer some colours but are scared off by others?

Other ideas:
- Save plastic mesh bags from supermarkets (often used for onions or oranges) and fill them with peanuts.
- Thread unshelled peanuts onto strings.
- Hang up fir-cones dipped in fat - soft lard or dripping - or spread with peanut butter. 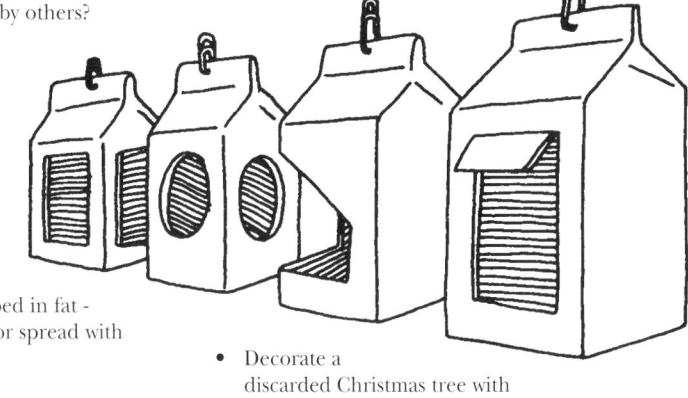
- Decorate a discarded Christmas tree with these fir-cones, strings of unshelled peanuts and your hanging bird feeders.

91
Help your child to learn

Young children find the concept of passing time difficult to grasp. They have no idea how long they have to wait for a birthday 'next year', a holiday 'next month' or a favourite TV programme 'next Tuesday'. You can help them develop a sense of time by talking about past events in their own lives, such as birthdays or holidays and telling stories about when you were young.

Marking time

Make a family time line in the form of a book.

Stick in photos of your child as a baby, on their first birthday, second birthday and now. Give it the title 'Look How I've Grown!'

What do they think they'll look like when they get bigger?

The best way for your child to learn about history and how times are changing is to hear it from the expert - you! All adults have stories to tell of when they were young and your child will learn a lot from listening to them

When I was young

Here's a few ideas of things you could do with your child to help them understand some of the similarities and differences between today and when you were young.

- Share your photo album. Dig out those embarrassing pictures of you as a child.

- Sing them songs you learned as a child.

- Play them records, CDs or even videos of music you liked when you were in your teens.

- Ask grandparents or older relatives to share their stories, too.

- Show your child something you've kept since childhood.

Physical Development

This area of learning is concerned with developing control, movement and coordination and helping children stay healthy and active.

- Young children can combine movements such as clapping hands or pointing to various body parts. Later on they will be able to carry out more coordinated movements such as threading beads or posting a letter.

- At first, your child will need help with fine movements such as doing up their coats. Later they will manage to do zips and buttons.

Children should be given opportunities to play with small and large equipment. Pushing a doll in a pushchair, for example, will help them gain a sense of space and direction. When playing throwing and catching, you may notice that a younger child may try but not be able to catch a ball or can kick a ball but not score a goal. With practice and experience they will be able to catch balls and begin to score goals.

Children need the chance to play in open spaces and explore what their bodies can do. You can go for walks together and even play simple games to help your child develop more control of their body and become confidently physically

Learning what bodies can do

Children need to know what their bodies are capable of and learn to control them.

To move confidently and safely they also need to develop an awareness of the space around them and how their movements affect others.

You can help them to develop this control and awareness, both indoors and outdoors. As often as possible go for walks with your child to a nearby open space, such as a park or field, where there is room to run and enjoy freedom of movement.

When the weather is too bad to go out, play simple games indoors which involve different movements.

Nursery rhymes
Think of suitable nursery rhymes to sing which involve different movements, for example 'The Grand Old Duke of York', 'Jack and Jill' and 'Ring a Ring of Roses'.

Jack and Jill went up the hill

To fetch a pail of water.

Jack fell down and broke his crown

And Jill came tumbling after!

Follow my leader
Find as large a space as possible to play this game. It can be played with one child or several. Tell children that you are going to go for a walk and they must follow behind, copying exactly what you do. Start with easy movements, such as stretching your hands up in the air, and gradually make them more complicated according to the age and abilities of the children. Once they understand the game choose someone else to be the leader.

Children need to learn how to control their bodies when they are still and moving. At your child's pre-school setting they will be doing activities to help them with this and you can help, too. It's all about learning what your body can do and knowing the words to describe it

Going on a bear hunt

Many rhymes can be used to introduce words to do with movement - over, under, through, around and across. Try saying 'The bear hunt' together. This rhyme not only focuses on over, under and through but also explores moving through different terrains - thick, squelchy mud, long, wavy grass and swirly, whirly water. You can add your own verses, for example: crunchy, crackly leaves, lumpy, bumpy road and slippery, slidey ice.

The Bear Hunt

Chorus:
Adult: We're going on a bear hunt!

Child: We're going on a bear hunt!

Adult: We're going to catch a big one!

Child: We're going to catch a big one!

Adult: We're not scared!

Child: We're not scared!

Adult: What a beautiful day!

Child: What a beautiful day!

Adult: Oh! Oh!

Child: Oh! Oh!

Adult: Mud

Child: Mud

Adult: Thick, squelchy mud

Child: Thick, squelchy mud

Adult: We can't go over it

Child: We can't go over it

Adult: We can't go under it

Child: We can't go under it

Adult: We'll have to go through it

Child: We'll have to go through it

Make slurping noises with your mouth whilst making slow, heavy footsteps on your knees.

Chorus:
Adult: We're going on a bear hunt!

Child: We're going on a bear hunt.......

Repeat as above for other terrains you might encounter on your journey, until:

Oh! Oh!

Adult: What's this I see?

Child: What's this I see?

Adult: Two black furry ears

Child: Two black furry ears

Adult: Two beady eyes

Child: Two beady eyes

Adult: And a great big mouth

Child: And a great big mouth

ALL: It's a bear!

Quick! Run back through the cave ... *(Repeat all the actions and noises in reverse)* ... into the house .... and close the door behind you with a great big BANG!

Children enjoy energetic, physical and free play. As they play they become aware of what they can do and what it is possible to do. As they move they are also learning the language of movement – the speed, direction and position of their movements

Learning words for actions

Fine days

When you take your child to the park or any other large open space, encourage their movements by suggesting the following:

- In a large open space encourage free movement – how fast or slow can they move? Can they move backwards and sideways as well as forwards? Can they change position – up and down as they move?

- When using apparatus in the park, encourage them to describe their position – are they at the top or the bottom of the slide? Can they crawl under or over the bars?

Useful words
fast/slow
up/down
in/out
over/under
to the right/to the left
forwards/backwards
inside/outside
on/in
under/over
top/bottom
high/low

Wet days

- Although space is limited inside don't let the weather put you off! Think of action songs – 'The Grand Old Duke of York', 'Jack and Jill', 'The Hokey Cokey'. All these will encourage your child to move in certain ways and help them understand the language used to describe movements. Board games such as 'Snakes and Ladders' and 'Ludo' also help with concepts such as before, after, up and down.

- Play a copying game – 'Follow my Leader' or 'Simon Says'. When your child is ready, let them take the lead and you do the copying!

The Grand Old Duke of York

Oh the grand old Duke of York

He had ten thousand men

He marched them up to the top of the hill

And he marched them down again.

And when they were up, they were up

And when they were down they were down

And when they were only half-way up

They were neither up nor down.

Help your child to learn

Balancing games or activities are one way of helping children gain greater control of their bodies. Physical activity helps to make children's bones and muscles stronger

Learning to balance

You don't need any special equipment - everyday objects can be much more fun.

1. Lay a washing line out on a flat surface, in a wiggly shape. Encourage your child to walk along the 'slippery snake'.

2. Walk along pavement markings/cracks.

3. Walk along low walls.

4. Encourage your child to walk around with different items balanced on their head, for example:
   - an empty plastic bowl
   - a plastic cup and saucer
   - a plastic bag filled with water and tied securely!

5. Increase the difficulty of activity 4 by encouraging the child to clap their hands when walking/march with high knees/walk backwards!

Combining activities 4 and 5 demands an even greater degree of control!

6. Place a piece of wood (about 30cm wide) on two stacks of house bricks, one brick high. Encourage your child to walk along the wood - hold their hand if they are unsure. As their confidence grows, raise the height of the wood by adding bricks to both ends.

The ability to balance is an essential part of the way children control their body movements. You can encourage your child to develop this skill as you play at home together. Bring favourite stories to life by acting them out and include opportunities for balancing

Goldilocks and the three bears

You can act out this story indoors or outdoors with imaginary props. Make it more exciting by pretending the space outdoors is the woods and your house is the house of the bears.

Begin by walking through the woods together.

- Stretch up on one leg to pick some blossom from a tree and smell it.
- Bend over to pick some flowers.
- Hop through some long grass.
- Jump over a stream.
- Crawl along on all fours under a log.
- Tip-toe up to the house.

Inside the bear's house mime the movements as you relate the story.

- Taste the bowls of porridge.
- Climb into Daddy Bear's high chair.
- Curl up in Mummy's middle-sized chair.
- Sit in Baby Bear's chair and rock backwards and forwards on your bottom as the chair breaks.

Climb up the stairs, emphasising how high each step is and try the three beds.

- Stretch up to climb into the high bed.
- Lie flat on the middle-sized bed and rock backwards and forwards to get up again.
- Curl up in a tight ball to sleep in the small bed.

Repeat the first actions quickly as Goldilocks runs back through the wood.

Even babies are developing balancing skills as they lift their heads, learn to sit up, pull themselves to a standing position and begin to take their first steps. By the time children start pre-school they are usually beginning to have more control over their movements. But their bodily control varies enormously. Some have no difficulty in climbing to the top of a climbing frame or balancing along a narrow beam. Others may be reluctant to venture from the safety of solid ground because they lack the skills and confidence.

You can help your child at home by giving them the chance to practise balancing skills such as those suggested in this game. Children get a lot of satisfaction and a sense of achievement from this aspect of their physical development.

If you have a large garden or are holding a birthday party in the local village hall, here is a game that will get children running, chasing, dodging and out of puff, ready for the food!

Party game

Snatch the tail off the donkey

1 Make some tails by cutting up strips of different coloured crepe paper about 7cm (2 - 3 inches) wide and 30cm (12 inches) long.

2 Each child tucks a tail into a pocket, sleeve, trouser, skirt or shorts waistband.

3 The farmer has to catch all the tails off the donkeys within the shortest time.

4 All the children take turns at being the farmer and the child who catches the most tails is the winner.

Note: If you are playing the game with a lot of children, split them into coloured tail groups. Half the group watches while the other half plays. Split each half into two colours and have two farmers to collect either all the red or all the blue tails.

Parachute play is a big favourite in some nurseries. It helps children learn to work together as well as developing muscles in their arms, chest and shoulders. At home you can improvise and have fun with a simple sheet

Make a simple parachute

Fun activities for you and your child

- Give a favourite teddy a ride by sitting it in the middle of the sheet, holding the sides and lifting them up and down to make the teddy bounce.

- Roll a soft ball around on the sheet and try to get it through the hole in the middle.

Activities for two or three children

- Let two children hold up the sheet while the third crawls underneath.

- Ask a child to sit in the middle of the sheet and get the other two to flap the sides.

- Have one child lying under the sheet while the others roll a ball around on the sheet above. See if the child can kick or punch the ball off the sheet from underneath.

1. Start with an old sheet.

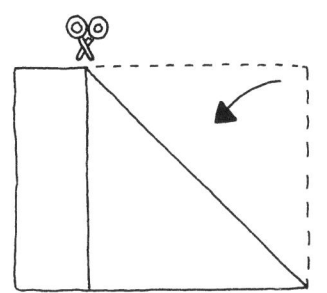

2. Fold as indicated and cut off surplus sheet.

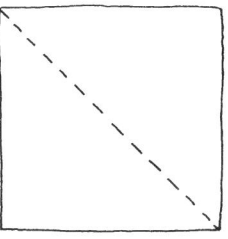

3. Open out to form a square.

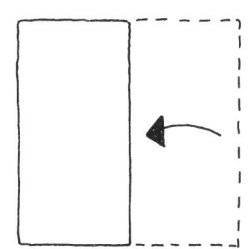

4. Fold once.

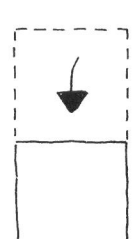

5. Fold again to form a small square.

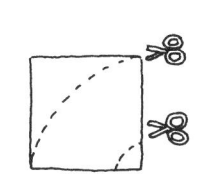

6. Draw lines as indicated.

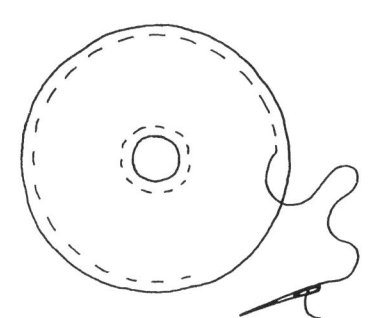

7. Open out to form the canopy. Hem to strengthen.

8. Add handles if required.

Help your child to learn

Hula hoops are inexpensive toys and can give hours of fun as children grow. Young children will not be able to spin a hoop around their waist but they can do it using their arms. (You may need a smaller hoop for this)

Hoop fun

Get your child to stretch out their arm and hang the hoop on their wrist.

Show them how to rock the hoop back and forth on their wrist.

Can they make it rock by themselves?

Lots of things to do with a hoop

How many ways can you pass through a hoop?
You can go feet first, head first, arms first - even bottom first!

How many people can stand in a hoop at the same time? Three children? One adult?

How 'long' is your hoop? Encourage the first steps in measuring by taking a piece of string and laying it around the hoop. Cut it to the right length and then hold it out straight. Then compare the length of the string with the height of your child - and yourself.

You might notice that the string is just over three times as high as the hoop!

When they can do this, get them to swing the hoop in a full circle by getting them to polish windows. They should make a circular movement of their outstretched arm from the shoulder - make sure this is not too big a movement by asking them to 'polish a small patch of the window'.

Children need to spend lots of time just playing with a ball before they can be good at rolling, throwing, catching and bouncing. Here are some games you can play with them to help

Ball games

Most homes have a selection of different size balls. Collect them up and let your child have some fun and improve their physical development at the same time. (Make sure you choose the right size ball for the experience of the child.)

Balls and walls
Play throwing and catching with a medium size ball against a wall. If you stand alongside your child and do it with them they can learn by watching how you do it. Or to begin with, they can throw and you catch.

Scoring goals
Hold a bucket and see if your child can throw the ball into the bucket. Because you can move the bucket to 'catch' the ball their confidence will build up as they 'score goals.' Try to move the bucket less and less to catch the ball. This will improve their hand-eye coordination.

Targets
Whether they are kicking, rolling or throwing a ball, give your child a target to aim at - your legs astride, a mark on the wall, a washing basket to throw into, skittles to knock down.

Catching can be taught but it takes practice. By covering a balloon with material you can create a ball that is fun to use and easy to handle. Here's how

Playing catch

A covered balloon has lots of advantages over a real ball: it is easy to pick up, it can be grabbed with one hand, it is light so children will not flinch away from catching it and it moves relatively slowly, which makes it easy to catch. Yet, unlike a balloon, it behaves like a real ball. Its weight means that it can be used indoors.

- First, choose your material - the more colourful, the better.
- Trace the pattern and use it to cut out six panels.
- Sew the edges together inside out.
- Next, sew the top of the casing together. Turn it the right way round, insert a balloon and inflate.

You can use the balloon in much the same way as you would an ordinary ball.

Give your child challenges.

- How many times can they throw and catch the balloon without dropping it?
- Can they beat their highest score?

Give them targets to aim at. Old boxes painted or covered with coloured paper are ideal and inexpensive. You can also paint numbers on the sides, which means you are not only helping with their physical development but also with their number recognition. Instead of numbers, try shapes.

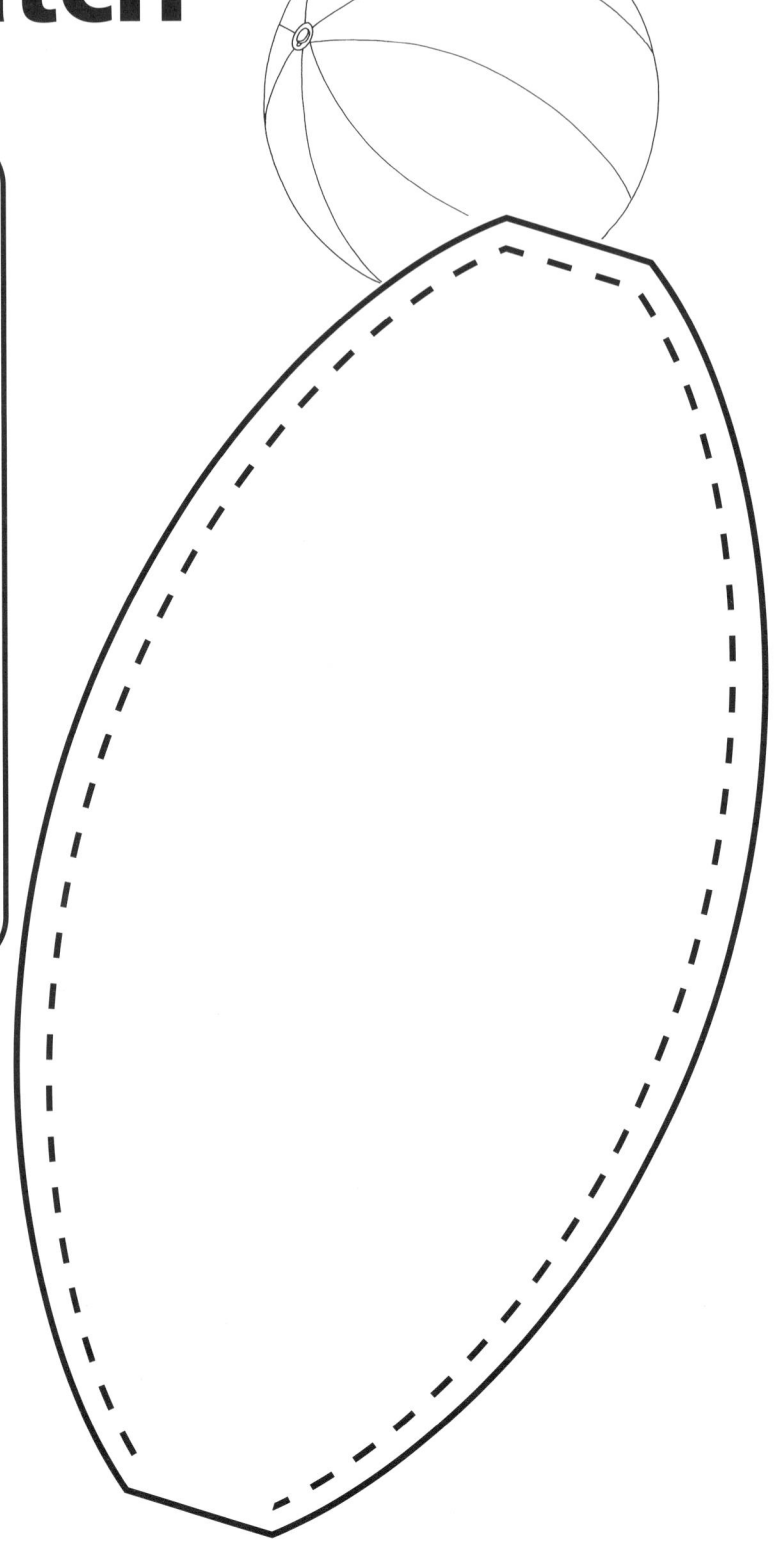

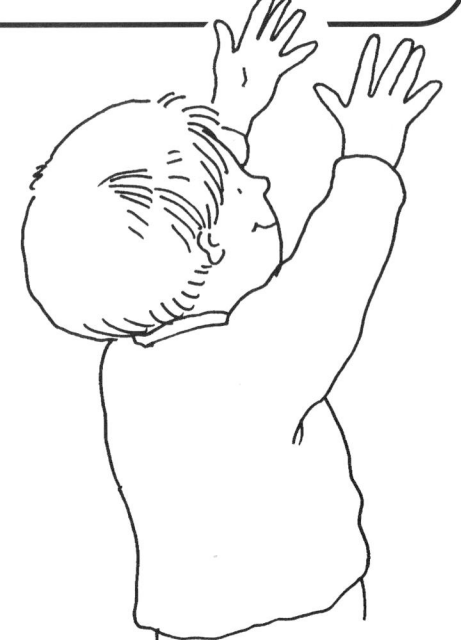

Use this game to help your child in their physical development - it's also an ideal way to help calm down an over excited child

Happy hands

Hands on hips

Hands on knees

Put them behind you (if you please!)

Touch your shoulders

Touch your nose

Touch your knees

And then your toes

Put your hands in front of you

Now let's clap them - one and two

Put your hands way up high

And let your fingers wave bye bye

> When playing with your child give them plenty of time and praise. Encourage them to come up with their own ideas. Use positive terms such as 'Let's try this way' rather than 'don't'. Make this a fun time together and you will both benefit.

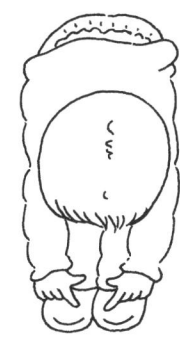

Increasing children's awareness of their own bodies is one of the first stages in developing coordination. With this game you can also introduce the concept of left and right

Simon says

An old favourite that encourages coordination skills is 'Simon Says'. Once your child is familiar with the rules of the game you can make the movements more and more complicated. Even walking down the street you can make big strides or small steps and at home the movements can involve bending and stretching, one arm up, one arm down, and so on.
The rules are easy:

- If you say 'Simon says do it' your child must copy the action you are doing

- If you say 'do it' without mentioning Simon, they don't copy

- If your child makes a mistake, they become Simon and the game continues.

Remember to give lots of praise and encouragement.

The more children explore the world around them the more skilled they become at using their hands. You can provide things for children to do at home which will encourage them to practise the skills they will need as they grow older

Using hands and fingers

Personal independence
Starting school is a worrying time for children and for parents. You can make the transition from home to school easier by encouraging your child to manage dressing and undressing on their own. At school, children will need to put on their coats to go outside and get changed for physical activities. Play games involving dressing dolls, preferably in clothes with buttons and zips. Have fun in races together putting on accessories such as hats, scarves and gloves. Look in the mirror at yourselves!

Helping at home
Let your child help with tasks around the house which involve handling small items. Set the table together, spoon out ingredients when baking, stir mixtures, turn the handle of a whisk, roll out pastry and cut out shapes. Give your child a small container with a duster, and a dustpan and brush, and enjoy some help with housework!
Encourage your child to help wash and dry the dishes by providing a small bowl and some warm water on a low table. Make sure that only safe dishes are used - no glasses or sharp edges. Children always enjoy polishing shoes and will take great pride in cleaning the shoes of other members of the family.

Shopping
Go shopping together and encourage your child to write a list beforehand, or draw appropriate pictures of items. At the shop let the child put things in the trolley or basket. Back at home put the shopping away together.

Gardening
Have fun growing things outdoors or on window sills. Children can scoop compost into yoghurt pots, poke holes in the centre and drop seeds in. They can then water these carefully.

Games to play together
There are many simple board games which involve throwing dice and moving counters. Children love to play these with an adult.
Play with buttons together. Sort them into lines according to size or colour, or thread them onto laces.

Fine motor skills
Encouraging children to develop their manual dexterity - or fine motor skills - is an important part of a child's pre-school education.

Children need to develop their manual dexterity in order to cope with their personal needs, such as dressing and keeping themselves clean.

Children who have enjoyed activities involving the exploration of a wide selection of tools and materials are more likely to approach drawing and writing with confidence.

Children need time to practise the movements they have already mastered and the chance to try out and repeat new ones.

Have you ever tried to use chopsticks? How much food did you manage to get from the plate into your mouth? Well, trying a new experience like that can make you realise how difficult unfamiliar physical activities are for young children

Cleversticks

Things that we take for granted, such as doing up buttons, threading needles and tying shoelaces, all need to be learned. These skills are part of children's fine motor development and it's important that learning them is made as much fun as possible.

You will need:
- two sets of chopsticks
- two plastic bowls
- a collection of small objects, for example:
  - lengths of knitting wool in a small bundle
  - cotton-wool balls
  - small sponge or foam shapes
  - dry pasta shapes
  - large wooden beads
  - small plastic bricks
  - a small soft toy (it may be a good idea to hunt for new items with your child)

Collect all the objects into one bowl. Talk about using the chopsticks. If you have been to a Chinese restaurant together, or you've eaten a Chinese take-away at home, talk about your experiences. Then talk about trying to pick up the objects using the chopsticks:
- Which will be easy?
- Which will be hard?
- What's a good way to hold the chopsticks?

Now it's time for the really fun part – take it in turns to try to move an object from one bowl to the other! When someone moves something into the bowl successfully, everyone calls out 'Cleversticks!'

Have lots of fun and laugh together when things fall off the chopsticks. Talk about ways of making it easier. When you've moved all the objects from one bowl to the other, talk about your ideas of things that would be easiest. Were you right?

If your child is still enjoying the game, move the items back to the other bowl. Now it will be a race to choose the easy things. When you've finished, think about other things you could move with chopsticks. Perhaps you could make another collection. Then talk about other ways of moving objects – using tweezers, sugar tongs or different sized spoons!

Young children need the time to explore with their hands, touching and feeling materials before moving on to more formal skills such as writing and drawing. Playing with dough is the perfect way to practise

Recipe for playdough

Try this recipe for long-lasting playdough:

225g/8oz plain flour

100g/4oz salt

30ml/2 tbsp cream of tartar

15ml/1 tbsp vegetable oil

225ml/8 fl oz water

A few drops of food colouring

Mix all the ingredients, except the colouring, into a smooth paste. Cook in a saucepan slowly over a low heat, stirring occasionally, until the dough comes away from the pan and makes a smooth ball. Remove and, when cool, add a few drops of food colouring, then knead.

This dough should last for a month or two when stored in an airtight container in a fridge.

Points to remember

- Involve your child in weighing and mixing the ingredients.
- Occasionally add extra ingredients such as cornflour, lentils or glitter to create different textures.
- Provide a variety of tools for your child, such as cutters and a rolling pin and items that will make an imprint, such as cotton reels, Duplo pieces and Sticklebricks.

Why is dough play valuable?

- Playing with dough leads to increased control of fine movements of the fingers and hands.
- It develops and exercises the muscles in the hands and arms.
- It gives children the chance to create and express their ideas and feelings in a safe way. There is no pressure to succeed and they can easily roll it up and start again!
- It gives children the opportunity to see what materials feel like and how they behave.

You want your child to feel good about themselves and to learn to take care of their own bodies. If they can achieve this at an early age then children grow into confident healthy adults

Feeling good and keeping healthy

- Enjoy a balanced diet with plenty of fresh fruit and vegetables. Have sweets, crisps and biscuits only as special treats.

- Encourage your child to manage at the toilet and wash their hands afterwards.

- Always ask your child to wash their hands before handling food.

- Encourage your child to clean their teeth, especially after eating something sweet.

- Have some form of vigorous exercise every day. Go for walks, a swim or visit the park. In bad weather enjoy exercise, such as dancing to music, indoors.

- Show your child how to cross roads safely and talk about what to do if they are lost.

- Emphasise dangers in the house, such as electrical appliances, open windows and stairs.

- Talk together about likes and dislikes.

- Make sure that your child has lots of choices and ask their opinions.

- Talk together about what makes you happy, angry or sad.

- Give lots of praise and encouragement.

- Make bedtime routines relaxed and happy to ensure a good night's sleep.

At school or pre-school your child will learn about some of the changes to expect when their body has been working hard. It's part of the early years curriculum

Learning how our bodies work

Throughout the day your child will be telling you how they feel. Explaining these feelings and suggesting reasons for them and solutions to any discomfort will encourage your child to become more independent and self-sufficient. Obvious though most of the answers sound in these examples, you will be pleased to know that your usual responses are useful and educational!

'Mummy, my tummy hurts'
'Your tummy hurts because it is empty and you are hungry. You need food!' or perhaps 'Your tummy hurts because you ate too much lunch too quickly. Next time you will know not to eat so much so fast!'

'I'm cold!'
'You're cold because you are not wearing your coat.'

'I'm out of breath!'
'You're out of breath because you have been running and your muscles have used up all the air. You need to breath in some extra air until they have enough.'

Explaining to a tearful and crotchety child that they are tired will not be popular at the time - especially if you then put them to bed! But making sense of feelings like tiredness does give your child a sense of reassurance and will eventually help them to recognise the signs for themselves - a great step forward for independence!

If your child owns a trike, then a few home-produced props will improve their imaginative play

Getting the best from ride-on toys

Children's play is influenced by experiences in their everyday life. If your child goes on regular car journeys, they will often relive these trips in imaginative play with their trikes.

Watch them as they ride - do they add sound effects to turn their trike into a car or ambulance? Ask them where they are going - is it only twice around the rose bush or are they reliving a trip to the supermarket?

A regular car journey is to the garage and you can recreate this at home. Most children will be familiar with petrol pumps, and it is simple to make your own.

Open the flaps on a cereal box, turn it inside out and then reseal it.

Cut a small window in the front and a hole in either side of the box at the same level, big enough to take the inside cardboard tube of a kitchen roll.

Take a cardboard tube, for example a kitchen roll, and write numbers that your child is familiar with, around an imagined centre line.

Slide the kitchen roll through the hole until the numbers are visible through the window on the front.

Now, by turning the kitchen roll, you and your child can check how much petrol is being put into the trike. A nozzle can be made by cutting the top from a conditioner bottle, the type with a handle, and attaching it to the cereal box via a length of rope.

A tool kit for trike maintenance can be improvised with kitchen utensils - wooden spoons and spatulas for spanners and a rotary whisk makes an excellent drill. Provide cloths and buckets of soapy water so that your child can clean their trike wheels while you wash your car.

Finally, a garage can be made from a large grocery box obtained from a supermarket - such boxes may also become fire stations, tractor sheds or even stables with a little imagination.

Learning to use scissors is a difficult skill to master and a child should always be supervised while using them. Child-sized scissors with rounded edges are the best and safest

Scissor happy!

When your child is just beginning to use scissors, the most important thing is gaining control. So give them a few thin strips of paper, about 20cm long and 1cm wide, to snip through. Provide a small container for the cuttings to drop into. Your child will enjoy sticking with these small pieces later.

Give lots of praise and encouragement and let your child repeat this simple snipping activity over and over again. Repetition and allowing plenty of time will give your child the confidence to attempt more complicated cutting, such as cutting out or around shapes.

Make a simple book together by folding large sheets of paper in half, hole-punch the top of each sheet and join the pages together with string or ribbon. Give your child a selection of old magazines and catalogues and invite them to cut round the pictures and stick on to the pages to make a book.

You can collect pictures on favourite topics such as cars, toys or cats. Collect pictures of different shaped objects for them to cut around, such as a round ball or a square box and stick these into a home-made book. Old birthday and Christmas cards are also excellent for this activity.

Place the finished book with your child's other books – it will soon become a favourite.

Which scissors to buy
Sharp scissors are important as children soon become frustrated when trying to cut with blunt ones. Round-ended scissors are safest and those with plastic handles are chunky so young children can handle them.

Make sure you have left-handed scissors if your child is left-handed. Try: Anything Left-Handed, suppliers of all kinds of left-handed products, including scissors.
Tel: 020 8770 3722 website: www.anythingleft-handed.com

Creative Development

Creative development is about exploring colour, texture, materials and sounds. Being creative also involves children using their imagination and their senses.

- **When they first start nursery or pre-school, children will be able to explore colour, for example, by using and mixing paints. They will play with musical instruments and move to music. Later on they will develop a sense of rhythm and sing simple songs from memory.**

- **A three-year-old will start to develop their imagination as they begin to take part in role play or play with dressing-up clothes. The play will become more imaginative as they take on roles or become characters such as a teacher, bus driver or mummy.**

- **Young children explore using all their senses, including taste, touch and smell. When they're helping you with the cooking, they will want to lick the spoon and touch the mixture. They will move on to being able to talk about what they see, hear, smell, taste or touch. Gradually, they will respond in a variety of ways. In taste, for example, they will know what they do and do not like.**

Young children love to explore with a pencil or wax crayon. The really enthusiastic ones will draw on anything - even the kitchen wall! Make the most of this early enthusiasm to help your child develop into a confident artist

From scribble to drawings

How can you help?
Put out pencils, wax crayons and coloured pencils in your child's pencil pot. Keep a supply of paper handy so that your child can draw whenever they want to. Start off with chubby pencils and crayons - they are easier for little hands to hold. Paper doesn't have to be expensive. At this very early stage, you can give them scrap paper but keep a supply of fresh paper for special drawings, particularly as your child gets older.

If you have room, it's also fun to have a blackboard on an easel and coloured chalks so they can explore drawing with different tools.

Early scribbles
Don't worry if your child seems to produce nothing but scribble. Gradually, the scribbles will grow into recognisable drawings as they develop more and more control over their pencil. These early drawing experiences are also useful preparation for when your child starts writing.

Put them on the wall
Show your child that you value their drawings by pinning them up on the wall. You could even choose one or two favourites to put in a clip frame. Encourage them to use their drawing skills by making birthday cards. Even the youngest child's work looks lovely when mounted on coloured card.

What is it?
When your child proudly presents you with a drawing, try not to ask 'What is it?' They may not yet understand that a drawing can be of something specific and the question will just confuse them. They will get to the stage of drawing people, animals, cars, even if they are the only one who can tell you what they have drawn! If in doubt, admire the beautiful colours they have used, or the interesting shapes.

Observational drawing
Once your child has been drawing recognisable things for a while, try asking them to look carefully at a particular object and draw what they see. This is called observational drawing. Choose something with a nice clear shape such as a leaf or a simple toy. If your child enjoys doing this, you can encourage them to choose their own objects to draw.

Save your favourites
Save your favourite drawings in a folder. You and your child will love looking back at early attempts - but make sure you add the date and name if you have other children!

Children take great pride and pleasure in the pictures they produce. This kind of work also teaches them to concentrate as well as developing visual skills

Drawing what you see

We all love our child's first attempts at painting or drawing - the blob with green and orange hair labelled 'mummy', the trees with purple leaves or the rainbow coloured houses. These imaginative interpretations of the world form an important stage in children's development. However, children also need to learn to see things as they really are and to look at things carefully.

Your child may already carry out close observation work in nursery or pre-school - it's where children are given an object and asked to draw or paint it. This may sound a tall order for four-year-olds, but the importance of the exercise is not so much in the actual painting but in the observation carried out before the painting begins. Children are encouraged to look at the object closely and talk about it. Only after this do they begin, with the clear aim of painting the object as it actually is and not as an imaginative response to it.

Why not try this out at home next time your child wants to do some painting? Let them choose what they'd like to paint - a pet, a bowl of fruit, some flowers, a favourite toy. Help them first by sitting down with them and asking some questions.

- What colours will you need to paint it?
- What shape is it?
- How big will you make it?
- What part will you start with?

To help your child learn to look closely at the things around them, you could cut out a simple cardboard frame (it can be rectangular, square or round). Let your child look through it and focus on something. You can do this inside or outside.

Let them find something that interests them - a toy, statue, park bench, swings - then get them to look carefully through the frame and draw what they see.

Next find something small - a ladybird, snail or a toy. Look at it carefully through a magnifying glass.
When they are ready, draw it. (When they have finished, put any living thing back into the garden.)

Young children love painting. Although your child will have lots of opportunity to paint at nursery or playgroup, painting is something they can also easily do at home

Brush strokes

Painting is a wonderful way of enabling your child to use their imagination. It also helps develop coordinated hand movements as they grip the brush and use it to spread the paint across the paper. It is something that even a young child can do on their own and you can hang their pictures on the wall or turn them into greetings cards. Most important of all, painting is great fun!

Try to give your child as much freedom as possible to explore the paint in their own way. Don't worry about the results – most children don't start to recognise that a painting can be of something until they are four or five years old.

If paintings are ending up a muddy brown, give your child just one or two colours to work with. Show them how to use different colours on different parts of the paper and how to wipe the brush on the edge of the pot to get rid of the excess paint. Otherwise, just leave them to get on with it. The most important thing is for your child to learn how to hold and use the paintbrush, to cope with the thick, liquid paint and generally enjoy themselves!

There are lots of ways of using paint, apart from simply painting a picture. Here are a couple of easy ideas that produce effective results:

■ **Floury paint patterns:** blend paint and flour to make a thick, runny mixture. Using a large brush, spread a layer of floury paint onto card and then draw squiggly lines and patterns into the paint. Leave to dry and use to make greetings cards, pictures or photo frames.

■ **Blending paint with cling-film:** drip blobs of two or three alternating colours in rows across the paper. Place a sheet of cling-film over the paper, press down gently and then pull the cling-film across the paper to blend the colours. This works particularly well with red and yellow to make a fire painting or a sunset.

What you need

All the materials you need for painting are cheap and easy to find in high street stores or art and craft shops. Look out for the following:

■ Non-spill paint pots
■ Thick brushes – one for each paint pot
■ Ready mixed paint in red, yellow and blue
■ Painting paper

Non-spill paint pots have a lid with a small hole for the paintbrush. The lids usually come in different colours to help the child see which colour paint is in the pot. Go for thick brushes, preferably with handles to match the colour of the lid and the paint.

A painting easel works well for young children but a table is also fine. Check that the table is low enough for your child to reach across.

Keep an old, plastic tablecloth to put on the floor and make sure your child is wearing old clothes. If the weather's fine, let them paint outside.

You can print with anything - natural or made - and make the most wonderful patterns or abstract pictures. There is no right or wrong way – whatever your child produces is their very own work of art

Printing with paints

Go on a hunt around your house and garden to see what interesting shaped objects – natural and made – you can find.

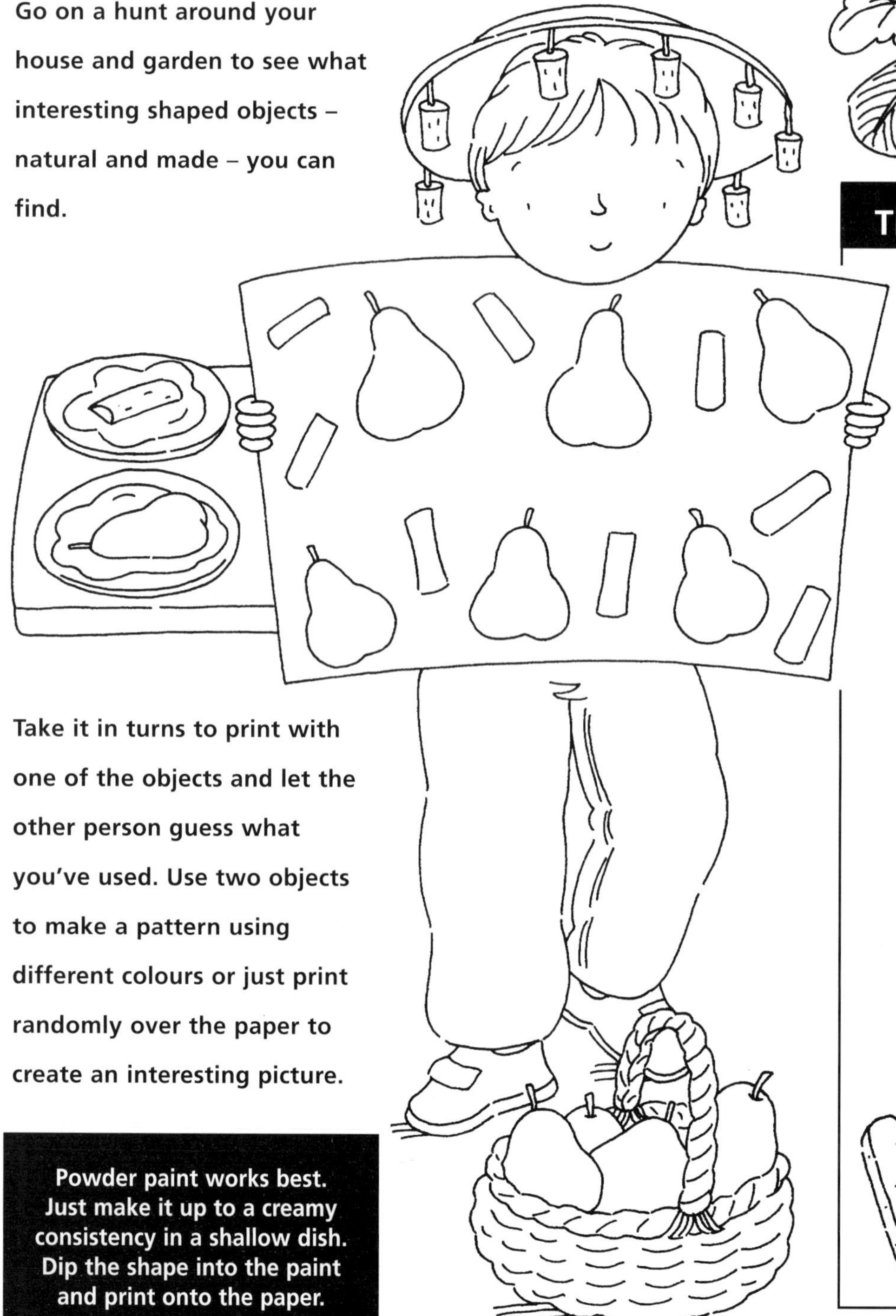

Take it in turns to print with one of the objects and let the other person guess what you've used. Use two objects to make a pattern using different colours or just print randomly over the paper to create an interesting picture.

Powder paint works best. Just make it up to a creamy consistency in a shallow dish. Dip the shape into the paint and print onto the paper.

Things to look for:

Cotton reels
Sticklebricks
Toilet roll tubes
Shells
Cones
Acorn cups
Biscuit cutters
Old toothbrush
Foam letters/numbers
Sponge
Wooden block
Bark
Leaves
Feathers
Fruit
Vegetables
Corks

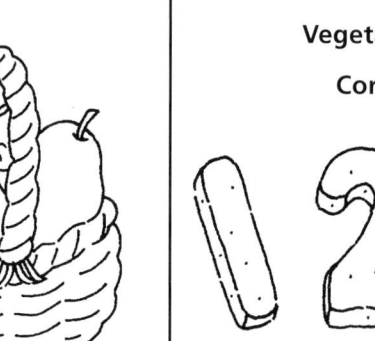

Wax crayons are cheap and easy to use. With their bright colours and chunky shape, they make an ideal early drawing tool for little ones

Using wax crayons

Starting off
At first, leave your child free to explore and enjoy the wax crayons. Choose chubby crayons to start off with and try to give them a range of different coloured papers to draw on. As your child becomes able to control the crayon and hold it firmly, you can start introducing some new ideas.

Different effects
Show them how to press hard, to make a strong, rich colour. Show them how to press lightly, to create a soft, shadowy effect and how to jab the crayon on the paper to make dots and flecks. Peel off the crayon's paper covering and show them how to use the crayon on its side. Give a little help if they are not yet strong enough to press hard. If they enjoy this, try cutting notches into the side of a chunky crayon to make a pattern.

Rubbings
Once your child is able to use the crayon on its side, they can make rubbings. Choose any object with a raised pattern. Place a piece of paper over the object and rub the crayon across to reveal the pattern. Experiment with objects such as pieces of bark, leaves or coins. Try using lots of different colours and turn the rubbing into a greetings card.

Making new colours
Two different colours can be used to make a new colour. Begin with a darker colour, such as blue. Show your child how to colour an area of the paper, pressing lightly. Colour over the blue with yellow, this time pressing hard. The two colours together will make green. You can then show your child how to draw onto the wax layer with a sharp pencil, revealing the blue underneath and creating an attractive pattern - another idea for turning into a card or picture.

Stained glass window
Give your child greaseproof paper to crayon onto. You can then tape the picture on a window - the sun shining through will make the wax colour glow like stained glass. Another technique is to crayon onto white typing paper and then paint over the back of the paper with cooking oil. Leave to dry before taping onto a window.

What to choose
If your child enjoys wax crayons, look out for different varieties - glitter crayons, fluorescent, gold and silver crayons, triangular and oblong shapes. Older children can explore thinner crayons and you can sharpen the points just like a pencil. It is possible to buy washable crayons if you have a little one who likes drawing on walls as well as paper!

As your child gets older, encourage them to try using just one or two colours - white and grey on a dark blue background or a dark green crayon on pale green paper. Experiment with the same colour on different coloured paper. A yellow crayon can look dull on white paper, bright and fluorescent on black paper. Talk about which effects you both prefer.

Help your child to learn

Cutting and sticking paper shapes onto backgrounds is fun and easy to do. It is great for making cards and calendars as well as pictures and patterns to pin up on the wall

Make a collage

Collage helps your child's development in all kinds of ways:

- making pictures from different papers gives them the opportunity to be creative;

- handling scissors and glue is good for the development of coordinated and controlled hand movements;

- an absorbing, hands-on activity, such as collage, helps your child's concentration to develop.

Getting started

Try making up a paper box for your child by saving scraps of wrapping paper, greetings cards, corrugated card from boxes, even little pieces of silver foil, Cellophane wrappings from sweets and sandpaper off-cuts. A variety of different papers will give your child lots of textures, colours and patterns to explore. Think about the difference between the texture of sandpaper and Cellophane, or the weight of card and tissue paper.

Introduce the different papers to your child one or two at a time. If you give them too many at once, it can be overwhelming. Try to offer two contrasting papers, such as tissue and card or wrapping paper and sandpaper. This will help them notice and explore the differences in texture.

Younger children will simply enjoy sticking paper shapes onto a background. As your child gets older you can encourage them to experiment with composition - do they prefer a shape at the bottom of the picture or the side of the picture, for example? They will also enjoy cutting out images from cards and magazines to use.

Cutting and gluing

If your child is ready to use scissors, show them how to hold them. Choose blunt-ended scissors designed for young children and always supervise. It is worth investing in the best you can afford as there is nothing more frustrating than scissors that don't cut.

If your child is not yet ready to use scissors, give them ready-cut shapes. This frees them up to concentrate on deciding where to put the pieces and gluing them on. Even older children won't be able to cut sandpaper or thick card by themselves.

You can use any non-toxic glue that is suitable for children (check the label carefully if a glue is not advertised as suitable for young children). A good choice is the white PVA glue sold in toy shops and stationers. You will need a little plastic glue spatula (easier to clean than a brush) although you will need to show your child how to put just a small blob of glue on the end of their spatula. Younger children find it easier to put a blob of glue onto their background and then place their shape on top of the blob rather than gluing the shape itself.

Tearing and crumpling

Tearing paper is an alternative to cutting and it creates an interesting edge. You will need a sheet of suitable paper and a heavy book that is longer than the paper. Place the book on the sheet of paper, leaving a strip of paper exposed. Press down on the book and show your child how to tear off a strip of paper. This can then be torn into smaller pieces or left as a long strip. Experiment with different types of paper - some tear better than others. You can also crumple up and then smooth out the torn strips to add another texture - this looks much more effective than it sounds and is fun to do. Try making striped or tartan patterns from the strips, or landscapes made up of layers of greens and blues.

The possibilities of collage are endless. As your child gets older and needs less help and supervision, sit down and make your own collage alongside them. This is a great way of relaxing and sharing ideas and inspiration. If your child sees you being creative, it will encourage them, and they will love the companionship of working with an adult.

This glittering stocking can be hung up as a decoration or turned into a Christmas card for friends and family

Fun with glitter and glue!

You will need: some thin white card or paper; red and green paint; some things to print with (polystyrene shapes, sponge stars, cotton reels); flat containers for the paint (with a thick layer of foam in each if you have any); PVA glue and a spreader; silver glitter; cotton wool; ribbon.

Your child will need to wear an apron or old clothes. Put plenty of newspaper on the table!

- Cut out some stocking shapes in advance to roughly A4 size (or cut circles or diamonds as decorations). Choose things to print with that have enough space for a good hand hold.

- Let your child dip the block into the paint. Show them how to scrape off any excess on the side of the container. Place the printing block down gently to get a good image. Let them choose their own shapes and patterns, making any arrangement they like. Talk about the different shapes, sizes and colours and about what we use Christmas stockings for or about decorations in general. Let the paint dry thoroughly.

- Put the stocking on a table covered with newspaper. Pick up the glue spreader and, holding it about 30cm above the stocking, let the glue dribble in a spidery pattern over the paint.

- Next, pick up small piles of glitter and cover all the dribbles thickly. Tip the stocking and tap it lightly to remove any excess and reveal the glittered lines over the bright paint. To finish off, dab a small amount of glue to the top edge of the stocking and carefully place some cotton wool on this. If it's to be used as a card, write a greeting on the back when it's dry and let your child add their name.

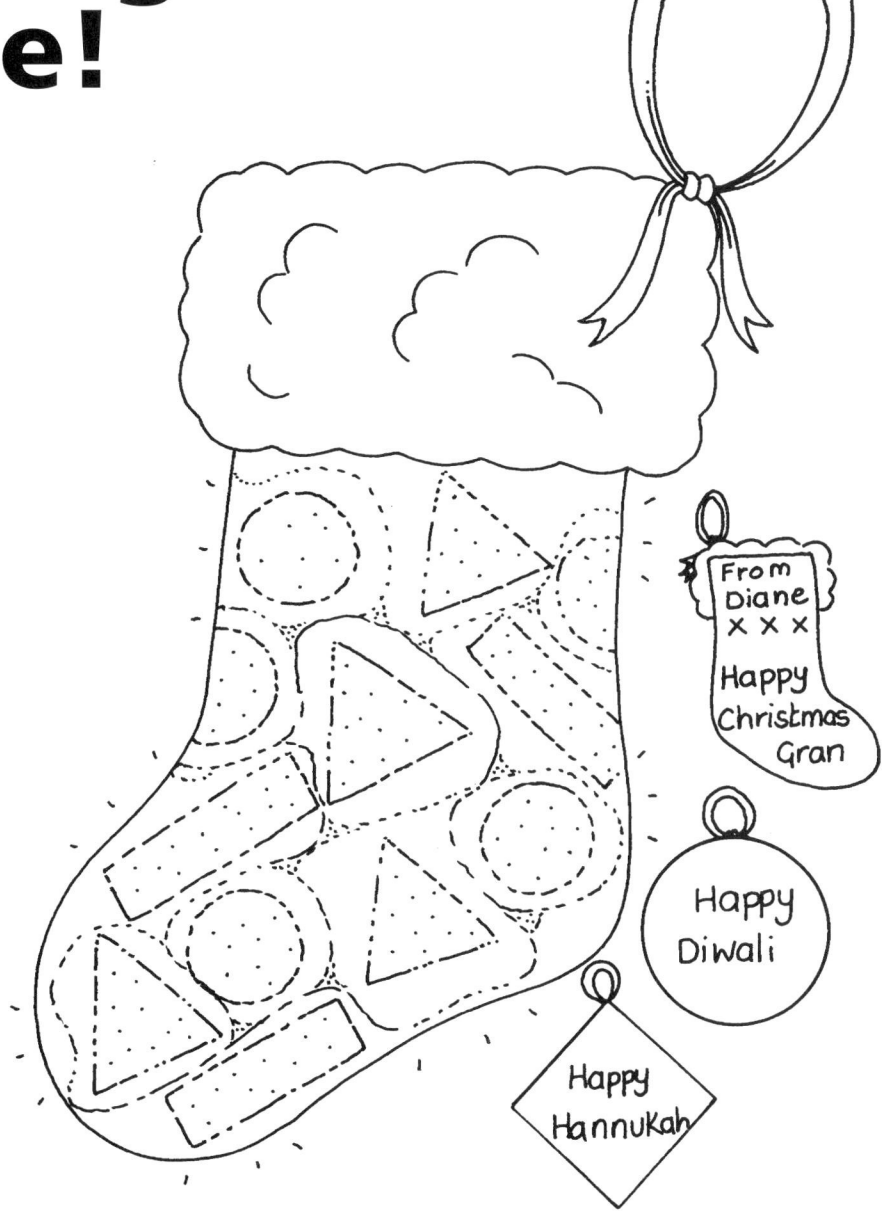

How this helps your child

This sort of art work, which has a series of steps to be followed, helps children develop their concentration. It is also a great opportunity to talk together. Help them name colours and shapes. The paint, glue, paper, cotton wool and glitter have such different textures - feel them and think of words to describe them.

Using a variety of small shapes, identifying tiny differences and similarities and then putting them on the stocking is a good pre-reading exercise. After all, words are made up of shapes.

Handling small printing items, dribbling on the glue and sprinkling on the glitter all goes to help develop the dexterity of their hands and that difficult skill of hand-eye co-ordination. In other words, the hand being able to do what the brain wants it to do. These small movements with the hands are called fine motor skills and once the child can match them to shapes they remember they can begin to write.

The educational value of puppets is enormous. Many educational television programmes use puppets. You can develop this with your own child without too much effort and you don't need any special or expensive materials

Puppets for fun

Through making the simplest of puppets, children are using a whole variety of skills such as planning, design, cutting, joining, handling tools and various materials, listening, memory recall, concentration and manipulation. They learn about size and shape. They have a chance to be creative.

Puppets also allow children to think out problems by acting them out in a safe environment. A child can relive an experience (good or bad) and give way to a fantasy.

Shadow puppets
You don't need to be good at drawing to make shadow puppets. You can cut out shapes, people, animals and objects from magazines as long as the outline is clear. Draw around stencils or use the stencils themselves by attaching a stick to the back. Use the wall as your screen, or even attach a sheet of greaseproof paper to a cardboard frame and place a torch or table lamp behind and you have the start of a shadow production.

Take some black card and cut out a crocodile's head (two pieces). Cut out the eye and nostril, attach a loop of elastic or card with glue to the two parts and place your two fingers of one hand through the loops. Take it to a light source and you have a sad crocodile with toothache (your arm becomes the creature's body). Now add another animal silhouette, a mouse maybe, and start to tell a story.

Lighting
Lighting could come from a torch, which children can use easily. An Anglepoise lamp or projector light is better as the light is much stronger.

Warning: these lamps get hot and adult supervision is advisable at all times when in use. Never place coloured Cellophane too close to a hot bulb as it will burn; use coloured bulbs.

Angle the light so that it is higher or lower than the puppeteers so that the performer's shadow is not seen. Experiment by moving the puppet towards the light source to make the shadow bigger.

Jointed puppets
Once you have mastered a single shape, try a puppet with moving parts. This is not as difficult as it sounds. By using a hole punch and paper fasteners you can make your puppet move. Draw the shape of a shark and a shark's jaw (see template). Cut them out and pin together using a paper fastener. Attach two rods with masking tape to both body and jaw and move the jaw stick up and down. You now have the perfect sea scavenger! Add a few more sea creatures and a seascape screen and another story unfolds.

Why not try out some of these creative ideas for using the senses to discover wood at home in the house, on walks and in the garden?

The wonders of wood

Looking at wood

- Look around the house for flat wooden surfaces, such as a table top, door frame or chopping board and look closely at the pattern of the grain of the wood. Can you see any knots? Put a piece of paper over the wood and rub it with a thick crayon. Can you still see the patterns in the rubbing you have made?

- Go for a 'wood finding walk' and look closely at fences, doors and the bark, roots and branches of a tree. Bring home some fallen twigs and arrange them in a vase. Ask your child to draw a picture of one of the twigs.

Smelling wood

- Collect together some wooden objects from around the house and bring in some twigs or logs from outdoors. Do they all smell the same?

- If you have a DIY enthusiast in the family, ask them if they will saw a piece of untreated wood. Let your child watch at a distance. Pick up some of the sawdust and smell it, but not too near to avoid inhaling the dust.

- Stand at a safe distance from a garden or allotment bonfire. Talk about the smell of wood burning. Does your child like the smell?

Touching wood

- Collect together some small wooden objects with smooth and rough surfaces, such as a piece of bark, a spoon, a twig and a toy brick. Put them in a pillowcase and take turns to feel something and guess what it is.

- Beg some wood off-cuts from a DIY enthusiast and sandpaper them until they are smooth. Use them to build houses and small pieces of furniture for dolls' house dolls. Talk to your child about how different the wood feels after sandpapering.

- Make a miniature garden in an old bowl filled with soil. Use wood off-cuts for small seats and stick twigs into the soil to create trees and bushes.

- Create unusual animals from corks, pushing in used match sticks for legs.

Listening to wood

- Lie under a tree on a windy day and listen to the creaking branches and rustling leaves.

- Watch someone working with wood and talk to your child about the different sounds made by hammering, sawing, drilling and planing.

- Cut an old broom handle into four pieces and sandpaper each piece until it is smooth to make two pairs of rhythm sticks. Knock them together in time to music.

- March to some music beating wooden chopping boards with wooden spoons.

- Walk beside a wooden fence while holding a stick against it. Talk about the different noises made by walking slowly or quickly.

Help your child to learn more about seeds at home: in the house, during shopping trips, on walks and in the garden

Sowing the seeds of creativity

Kitchen explorations
Search for seeds in kitchen cupboards. Show your child nutmeg, dried peas, lentils or beans and sift through a packet of muesli for sunflower seeds. Show them grains of rice or barley and point out the peppercorns in a pepper mill.

Cut up some fruit from the fruit bowl and take out the pips.

Explain that all of the things they have been looking at are seeds which will grow into new plants. Encourage them to handle them and talk about how they look, feel and smell.

Shopping expeditions
Search the shelves in supermarkets for small jars of seeds, such as coriander, cumin or sesame, and compare these to a large coconut. If possible, buy some of the more unusual seeds and crush them for your child to smell.

When you next visit a garden centre, look at packets of seeds. Explain that the picture on the packet shows what the seeds inside will look like when they have grown into plants. Buy some mustard and cress seeds to take home to grow and some seed to feed garden birds.

Walks in the woods
Collect seeds, such as conkers, acorns and sycamore keys. Sort them into piles of the same seeds. Make a plain dough mixture (see right) and create interesting patterns by sticking the seeds into the dough.

Put some small seeds into one empty yoghurt pot and some large seeds into another. Cover the top with a piece of material secured with an elastic band. Shake the pot up and down and compare the sounds you make.

Basic dough recipe
200g plain flour
100g salt
2 teaspoons cream of tartar
1 tablespoon cooking oil
300ml water
food colouring (optional)

1. Mix the flour, cream of tartar, oil and salt in a pan. Add the food colouring to the water, if desired.
2. Gradually add the water to the pan until the ingredients are thoroughly mixed.
3. Heat the mixture gently, stirring constantly. Continue to stir until the dough is stiff and then remove from the heat.
4. Tip out the dough onto a pastry board and allow to cool before kneading well.
This dough will keep well in the fridge for several weeks, wrapped in cling-film.

Garden seed searches
In spring, encourage your child to plant seeds in a small plot or container in the garden. Later in the year, collect seeds from garden flowers and sort them into types. Put individual seeds on a piece of white paper and try drawing or painting pictures of them.

Next time you go to the beach with your child, have a look for shells and interesting pebbles. Once you have a good collection, they can make a sea-shell plaque. It's a great way to display your finds and works well with any age group

Making a sea-shell plaque

You will need
A board or flat surface; Plasticene in a colour that sets off the shells; a biscuit cutter; thick card; thin ribbon; white PVA craft glue.

What to do
Press a ball of Plasticene onto a board to make a pancake about 1 cm thick. Using a biscuit cutter, cut out a shape and then turn over the Plasticene plaque to reveal the smooth surface underneath.

Show your child how to press their sea-shells into the Plasticene, using the thumb and index finger. Check that the shell has been pushed in far enough so that it doesn't fall out and help them if you need to.

Older children could make patterns, choosing shapes, sizes and colours to make them. They could draw grooves into the Plasticene to use as guidelines. Stars and circles make a good starting point.

Once the plaque is finished, brush over with craft varnish for a high gloss finish. Alternatively, mix one tablespoon of white PVA craft glue with two tablespoons of water and let your child brush the mixture over their plaque. Don't worry if the plaque is swamped with white liquid! It will dry to a nice clear finish.

When the varnish has dried, glue some card to the back of the plaque with PVA glue. The easiest way to get the right shape is to draw round the inside of the biscuit cutter before cutting out. Add a little loop of ribbon and you have a pretty plaque to hang on the wall – a memento of your holiday or a present for granny!

Finding shells
Apart from finding shells on the beach, you can also buy cheap bags of shells from many seaside shops. If you are not going to the beach yourselves, listen out for any friends and relatives who are heading to the seaside. Ask them to collect some shells for you.

What will your child learn?
Pressing shells into Plasticene enables your child to make a shell collage without having to glue awkward shapes. Younger ones can simply enjoy handling the shells (good for hand/eye coordination). Older ones can create interesting patterns.

Go for a walk in the park, find a few treasures, sort out some dried pasta from the kitchen cupboard and you can help your child make a dream catcher to hang from the window

Sweet dreams

Collect autumn leaves, conkers, seeds, acorns, feathers and so on. Back at home you can prepare the materials for your child to use. Select small coloured leaves and make a hole near one edge with a hole punch. If possible, make holes in some of the seeds and conkers so they too can be threaded.

You will need:
Paper plate; autumn leaves, seeds and small feathers (alternatively, you can cut leaf shapes out of red, orange and yellow card and buy packs of feathers from craft shops); pasta tubes; beads; silver foil; thread or string; wool; hole punch; scissors.

What to do:
- Cut the centre circle out of the paper plate to make a ring. Make up to eight holes around the edge using a hole punch.

- Weave lengths of different coloured wool through the holes and across the ring to make a web.

- Cut eight shorter lengths of thread or string about 15 - 20cm long.

- Thread the pasta, beads, silver foil, leaves and seeds onto each string.

- Fasten a feather on the end of each string with a knot.

- Hang a decorated string from each hole.

- Hang the dream catcher from the ceiling in your child's bedroom.

Dream catchers
Although the dream catcher legend varies from tribe to tribe, Native American dream catchers are said to protect sleeping children from nightmares. Bad dreams are caught in the web and fade with the morning light, while good dreams slip through the holes and into the sleepers mind. Read a picture book such as *Dream Catcher* by Audrey Osofsky (Orchard Books) to find out more about the legend.

Children don't need expensive toys to keep them happy - a box of old buttons can provide hours of fun! You can even bake your own button biscuits with this simple recipe

Buttons to bake

Collect as many different buttons as you can from old clothes. Put them into a box, so that you and your child can look at them and feel the different textures, shapes and sizes of the buttons. They can play with them, sorting them out and finding all the pink ones, all the white ones, all the unusual shapes, ones with two holes, ones with four holes.

- Look for buttons around your home. Where did you find them? Look for other fastenings. How many can you find? Are certain fastenings used for particular jobs?

- Talk about what buttons are used for. Why are they useful?

- Feel the different textures of the buttons. How do they feel different? How do they feel the same?

- Follow the recipe for button biscuits. Let your child help with measuring out, mixing, cutting and decorating the biscuits. Even if they are not as neat as yours it is important for them to do things themselves.

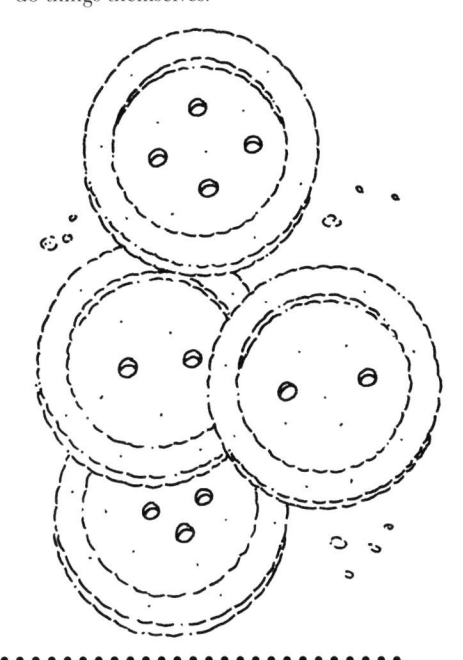

Safety note
Don't leave very young children on their own with buttons - they may put them in their mouth and choke.

Recipe

You will need
100g butter
100g caster sugar
1 large egg
225g plain flour
vanilla essence
(If your child has a dairy, gluten or egg allergy, use the same amount of dairy free spread, gluten-free flour or egg replacer given in the recipe.)
When the biscuit dough is made, leave it in the bowl for about 20 minutes before rolling it out. Don't put it in the fridge as this will make it too difficult to work with.

What to do
Wash your hands and put on an apron. Put on the oven at gas mark 4 or 180 C for electric ovens. Grease the baking tray with a little oil.

Weigh out the ingredients. Put in the sugar and fat and mix together. Mix in the egg and vanilla essence. Mix in the flour. This will make a stiff dough. Roll and cut out as many round biscuit shapes as you can. Use a smaller cutter turned upside down to make a rim shape and then use something small and round to make two or four holes or marks in the middle of the button biscuit. Put them onto the greased tray and bake for 15 minutes.

When the biscuits are cool, sieve a little icing sugar over the top to decorate or ice them and use small jelly sweets instead of the holes.

No doubt when your child was a baby you rocked and sang to them. You are still the most important person in your child's life and there are many ways you can enjoy music with them and foster an enthusiasm and love they will never lose

Making music

Movement: You don't have to be a professional dancer to enjoy a good boogie! Sing action songs together like 'Heads, shoulders, knees and toes'.

Understanding: Music can help a child to understand the world around them. Sing songs about everyday activities, for example 'This is the way we drive the car/wash our face/ jump in the puddles'. Music can also help children learn more about other cultures.

Sharing: At nursery or school, children learn to share by taking turns with instruments. At home you can share your favourite music with your child and they can teach you songs from nursery.

Instruments: Children love musical instruments. Invest in one or two or make your own.

Confidence: Singing and playing musical instruments increases confidence in young children. You don't need to be a trained musician to sing to your child with confidence they will copy you, not criticise you!

Interesting: Music can make everything seem more interesting. Make up your own words to familiar tunes about the people and places in your child's life.

Singing: Make singing part of your life. Not by joining a choir, just enjoy singing in the house. Don't worry if your child doesn't sound very tuneful - this is normal at their stage of development.

Fast/slow: Music is played at different speeds or tempos. Sing songs slowly then quickly. Try the same thing with clapping, stamping, and so on.

Universal: Music really is for everyone and there are so many kinds to discover. Children often love jazz and classical music. See what you can find in your collection.

Noisy/quiet: This is another important feature of music - the technical term is dynamics. Watch how your child responds to loud and quiet music. Which do they prefer? Do they enjoy tapping a cup with a spoon quietly as much as loudly?

x is for... xylophone!

Children will love making up their own simple tunes to play on this basic xylophone. Colour coding the bars enables them to describe their tune. If you help them to write it down in the same colour felt-tip pen - one red note, two blue, one red, for example - they can play it back, like a real composer! Make two and you can copy each others' tunes!

To make the xylophone:
You will need:
- Some chipboard for the base. Chipboard is availabe in all DIY stores - you may be able to buy a cheap off-cut. An oblong piece about 10 x 5 inches is about the right size.
- Two oblong strips of wood (about 8 x 2). Stick them to the base with super glue and then cover in draught excluder.
- Make a beater from two dolly pegs stuck together with insulating tape.
- Stick red and blue unsulating tape round the outside of the base to make the edges safe and attractive. 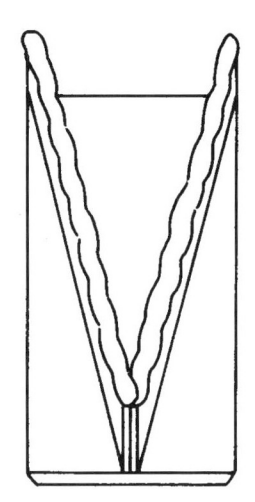 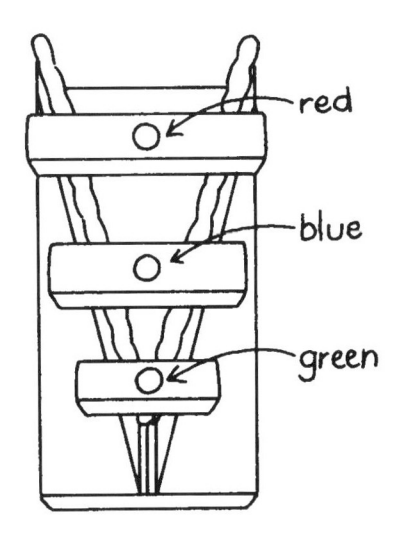
- Three different sized strips of wood (say 8, 6 and 4 inches long), sanded and colour coded red, green and blue with felt-tip pen. Place them freely on the base. (If you don't stick them down your child can move the notes around.)

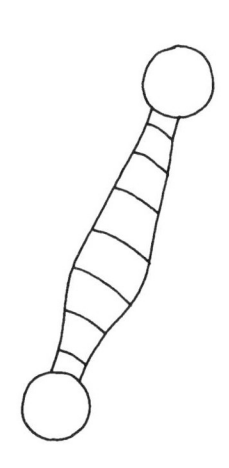

Don't throw those cartons away!

Make a drum from a large margarine pot covered with brightly coloured insulating tape.

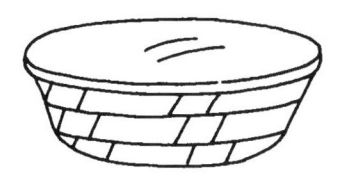

Make a shaker from a yoghurt pot. Fill it with things to make different sounds - split peas, shells, sand, pasta shapes, buttons - let your child choose. What makes a loud sound? What makes a soft sound? Cover the top with plastic and strong insulating tape so that they can't open it. You can do the same with clear plastic drinks bottles.

Wrap elastic bands around an old shoe box. Pluck the bands to make a sound.

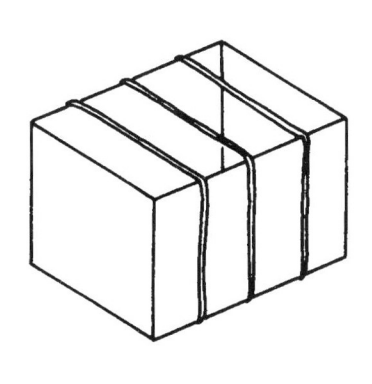

This simple cardboard box drum is easy to make

Make your own drum!

You need:
- Cardboard box
- Ribbon or long scarf
- Paint or stick-on decorations
- Tape and scissors
- Two wooden spoons or hazel sticks cut from a hedge or broom handle cut into four pieces (two sets).

What to do:
1. Tape up the top of your box.
2. Cut off folded flaps at bottom.
3. Cut two slits in the top; one at each side.
4. Thread ribbon through - long enough to go around back of neck (tie knot inside box).
5. Paint and decorate box .... PLAY!

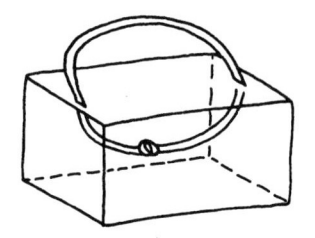

Children love to play on pots and pans in the kitchen - but why not arrange a whole band? You could use a set of saucepans on the ironing board at its lowest level. Hang spoons, a cheesegrater and whisks from a clothes airer. (Clay plant pots are also good - thread a stick attached to a piece of string through the hole to hang it up, bell like. Put lots in a row!) Put a big biscuit tin on a chair, an upturned waste bin or plastic bowls and buckets on the floor to one side.

Surround yourself with sound, using metal and/or wooden spoons as beaters!

When you teach your child to do the actions to favourite nursery rhymes you might not think of it as acting or drama, but in a way it is. You are encouraging your child to be creative and to use their body to express themselves in different ways

One, two, three, four, five

Poems and rhymes can be used to inspire imaginative and dramatic play in young children. At home, nursery rhymes are often the most useful, accessible source of poetry, familiar to us and our children. Try learning this rhyme with your child - the proper version first! Sing along if you know the tune. Encourage them to say the words as clearly as possible.

One, two, three, four, five,
Once I caught a fish alive;
Six, seven, eight, nine, ten,
Then I let it go again.
Why did you let it go?
Because it bit my finger so!
Which finger did it bite?
This little finger on the right!

Now try this version which has added drama! You and your child can choose where the fish has bitten you and act it out accordingly, the more dramatic the better!

One, two, three, four, five,
Once I caught a fish alive,
Six, seven, eight, nine, ten,
Then I let it go again.
Why did you let it go?
Because it bit me here you know.
Where did it bite you dear?
Here, here, here and here!

Starting school

Your child's playgroup or nursery will be preparing your child for 'big school', but they provide a great deal more support and have higher staff ratios than most Reception classes.

If you are worried about what might happen in school - or if you have any special concerns regarding your child - let the nursery or playgroup know. They should be able to give you guidance.

A child's first term at school can be a difficult time for all members of the family. Here are some ideas on what you can expect and what you could do to help

How to help your child

Some four-year-olds become exhausted when they first start school. This tiredness can be responsible for temper tantrums, bed-wetting, nightmares and other changes in behaviour.

Falling asleep as they go home or when they get there can disrupt meal times and postpone bedtime routine, all of which will lead to more anxiety and tiredness for both of you. It needs gentle understanding, lots of cuddles and encouragement and a quiet chat with the teacher who will welcome the opportunity to know she can try to help. If you feel that your child is not coping well talk it through with the teacher and see what arrangements can be made.

It helps if a child is quite independent when they start school.
There may be just two adults to 30 children in their class so your child will need to feel confident enough to manage by themselves. Areas where this is especially important are being able to use the toilet and wash their hands without help, and being able to dress themselves for PE or to put their coat on to go outside.
Encourage your child to be as independent as possible when dressing and at meal times. Let them pour their own cold drinks and look after their friends, brothers and sisters. Get them used to putting their toys away in the correct place. They will be expected to in school.

They will need to be able to listen and to recognise their own name. To help them do this
- play games which involve listening, such as I-spy
- encourage listening to music - perhaps play a tape of a new song
- talk with them about the activities they have done during their playgroup or nursery session.

When the time comes for the transfer, the most important way of relieving any worry is for your child to see where they are going and who they are going to be with.
The more times they can visit the school, the more confident they will become.
These visits will help to prepare you and your child for what's ahead. You can discuss with the teacher any fears that you might have and what your agreed approach will be if your child does not settle easily.
You will feel much more confident if your child does get distressed if you know what options might be possible in these circumstances.
Your child will also be reassured to know that their parent has a developing relationship with the grown-up who cares for them in school.

Are you worried about how your child will cope in the school playground? Is your child anxious about what to expect? Here are some ways to help your child make the move from nursery to school a happy one

Preparing for playtime

Before your child starts school
Before your child starts school, take them to see playtime. If possible, stand outside the school gates and let them watch from a distance. You may not be able to see the children, but voices and laughter will be heard.

You can also:

- Talk to your child about playtime. Discuss who they will play with and what they would play.

- Talk about what happens when playtime finishes and how they will know.

- Tell your child stories about going to school and playing in the playground.

- Share books together about school.

If your child has the chance to go to induction sessions, spend some time in the playground showing them the different areas.

If you go to a parents' induction evening, ask about playtimes. Ask where the children play. Is the whole school together? Is there any equipment to play with? Ask what happens at the end of playtime. Is a whistle blown or bell rung? Do children stand still or line up?

The more information you have the more you can tell your child. In this way there will be no surprises and your child will be more likely to cope with playtime from the beginning.

Invite friends to play who will be in the same class. If you don't know any other children in the school before the beginning of term then do this in the first couple of weeks.

Ask your child on a regular basis about their playtimes and if your child is unhappy:

- Try to find out why they do not like playtimes.

- Tell their class teacher.

- Ask that the lunchtime supervisors be told and make a time to speak to the teacher again to see if the situation has improved.

- Talk to other parents and perhaps pair up other children.

- Talk to your child about friendly behaviour, talking to a friend, sharing something, waiting for a friend after lunchtime.

- Explain about playtime rituals like the friendship stop.

Lunchtime
- If your child takes a packed lunch do not give them too much food.

- Only give food they like - this is no time to experiment.

- Make sure they can open their lunch box and put away their bag.

- If your child stays for a cooked meal, make sure they are used to sitting at a table to eat.

- Make sure they can use a knife and fork (or other children may make fun).

- Encourage them to put their hand up if they need something (play this as a game at mealtimes at home).

- Tell them not to get upset if they spill their drink. Encourage them to eat then go out to play with their friends.

- Encourage older siblings to look after brothers and sisters for part of playtime.

Every child in England and Wales is assessed when they first join a Reception class. Here we give you an idea of what this means, what to expect, plus tips to help you and your child deal with it

A guide to baseline assessment

What are the assessments for?
During the first half-term that your child is in Reception, teachers will carry out baseline assessment. They do it to find out what your child is currently able to do. They can then plan for their future learning on the basis of this information.

What do children have to do?
There are many different baseline assessment schemes in use across the country. Some are based on observation of children during everyday activities in school, while others involve children carrying out specific tasks. Some schemes are a mixture of the two. All schemes have to assess children in the areas of language and literacy, mathematics and personal and social development.

Because the assessment is normally made to seem like part of an everyday classroom activity, your child may not even know that they are being assessed.

What do you have to do?
Baseline assessment is not a test that children either pass or fail. It is a way for the teacher to get to know your child. You do not need to prepare your child for this process. It is far better for your child's teacher to find out what he or she can do without any prior help, and plan appropriate teaching on the basis of this.

How can you help?
The best way to help your child to make a confident start to school is to make learning a natural and enjoyable part of growing up. You can do this in many ways, for instance by sharing books with them in a way that is relaxed and fun. You could take your child to the local library, or take advantage of schemes operating at health centres in some parts of the country where books are on loan. Many things you may do already, such as talking together and playing games. Make the most of everyday situations and routines - weighing food or counting eggs when cooking, playing with water at bath time.

When you first visit your child's school or when your child has started Reception, the teacher will be able to tell you about the scheme that the school uses.

What happens afterwards?
After baseline assessment, the teacher will tell you about your child's performance. Remember that this will not be a report of pass or fail – there is no such thing in baseline assessment. However, what the teacher will tell you is where your child will be going next in his or her learning and how you can help your child progress.

The best way to help your child to make a confident start to school is to make learning a natural and enjoyable part of growing up.